CCCC STUDIES IN WR
Edited by Steve Parks, L

The aim of the CCCC Studies in Writing & Rhetoric (SWR) Series is to influence how we think about language in action and especially how writing gets taught at the college level. The methods of studies vary from the critical to historical to linguistic to ethnographic, and their authors draw on work in various fields that inform composition—including rhetoric, communication, education, discourse analysis, psychology, cultural studies, and literature. Their focuses are similarly diverse—ranging from individual writers and teachers, to work on classrooms and communities and curricula, to analyses of the social, political, and material contexts of writing and its teaching.

SWR was one of the first scholarly book series to focus on the teaching of writing. It was established in 1980 by the Conference on College Composition and Communication (CCCC) in order to promote research in the emerging field of writing studies. As our field has grown, the research sponsored by SWR has continued to articulate the commitment of CCCC to supporting the work of writing teachers as reflective practitioners and intellectuals.

We are eager to identify influential work in writing and rhetoric as it emerges. We thus ask authors to send us project proposals that clearly situate their work in the field and show how they aim to redirect our ongoing conversations about writing and its teaching. Proposals should include an overview of the project, a brief annotated table of contents, and a sample chapter. They should not exceed 10,000 words.

To submit a proposal, please register as an author at www.editorialmanager.com/nctebp. Once registered, follow the steps to submit a proposal (be sure to choose SWR Book Proposal from the drop-down list of article submission types).

SWR Editorial Advisory Board

Steve Parks, SWR Editor, University of Virginia
Chanon Adsanatham, Thammasat University
Sweta Baniya, Virginia Tech
Kevin Browne, University of the West Indies
Shannon Gibney, Minneapolis Community and Technical College
Laura Gonzales, University of Texas-El Paso
Haivan Hoang, University of Massachusetts-Amherst
Stephanie Kerschbaum, University of Washington
Carmen Kynard, John Jay College of Criminal Justice
Staci M. Perryman-Clark, Western Michigan University
Eric Pritchard, University at Buffalo
Tiffany Rousculp, Salt Lake Community College
Khirsten Scott, University of Pittsburgh
Kate Vieira, University of Wisconsin–Madison
Bo Wang, California State University

well done
beautiful

Living English, Moving Literacies

Women's Stories of Learning between the US and Nepal

Katie Silvester

Indiana University Bloomington

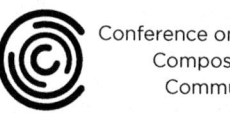

Conference on College Composition and Communication

NCTE National Council of Teachers of English

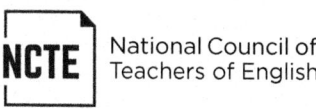

National Council of Teachers of English
340 N. Neil St., Suite #104, Champaign, Illinois 61820
www.ncte.org

Staff Editor: Cynthia Gomez
Manuscript Editor: Leigh Scarcliff
Series Editor: Steve Parks
Interior Design: Mary Rohrer
Cover Design: Pat Mayer

ISBN 978-0-8141-0170-4 (paperback); ISBN 978-0-8141-0171-1 (ebook)

Copyright © 2024 by the Conference on College Composition and Communication of the National Council of Teachers of English.

All rights reserved. No part of this publication may be reproduced or transmitted in any form or by any means, electronic or mechanical, including photocopy, or any information storage and retrieval system, without permission from the copyright holder. Printed in the United States of America.

It is the policy of NCTE in its journals and other publications to provide a forum for the open discussion of ideas concerning the content and the teaching of English and the language arts. Publicity accorded to any particular point of view does not imply endorsement by the Executive Committee, the Board of Directors, or the membership at large, except in announcements of policy, where such endorsement is clearly specified.

NCTE provides equal employment opportunity (EEO) to all staff members and applicants for employment without regard to race, color, religion, sex, national origin, age, physical, mental or perceived handicap/disability, sexual orientation including gender identity or expression, ancestry, genetic information, marital status, military status, unfavorable discharge from military service, pregnancy, citizenship status, personal appearance, matriculation or political affiliation, or any other protected status under applicable federal, state, and local laws.

Every effort has been made to provide current URLs and email addresses, but because of the rapidly changing nature of the web, some sites and addresses may no longer be accessible.

Library of Congress Control Number: 2023947454

I have no doubt that we must *learn to learn* . . . through the slow, attentive, mind-changing (on both sides), ethical singularity that deserves the name of "love."
—Gayatri Chakravorty Spivak, *Imaginary Maps: Three Stories by Mahasweta Devi*

CONTENTS

Acknowledgments ix

Prologue: *Angrējī BhāSā PaDhnu Bhanēkō Yastai Hō!* / "Learning the English Language Is Like That!": Susmita xiii

Introduction: Starting Places: Language and Literacy Learning between Pre- and Post-Resettlement Contexts 1

Part I: Speaking with/to: "Living-English" Stories 27

1. *Siknē Icchā* / "The Desire to Learn": Susmita 32

2. *Ma Aphnaī Lāgi Sikchu* / "I Learn for Myself!": Suk Maya 39

3. *(Malaaī) Ali-Ali (Angrējī) Āuchha* / "Just a Little (English) Comes (to Me)": Kali Maya 44

4. *Go Thalā Bhōkalā Māralā* / "The Hungry Shepherd Died": Abi Maya 49

5. *Gharkō Sukha-Dukha Jastai Hō* / "(Learning English) Is Just Like the Joys and Sorrows of Home": Kausila 54

6. Storyteller Learning and Doing / "Listening Back": Katie 59

Part II: Learning to Learn: Situating Stories across Languages, Locations, and Time 71

7. *Hāttī PaDhēra Thulō Hudaina* / "Elephants Don't Get Big by Reading": Literacy Presence from Stories of Absence across Resettlement Locations 75

8. *Hāmī Khēlchaū Sangīnī* / We Sing and Dance Together as Friends: Literacies on the Move and in Sensuous Coalition 93

9. Conclusion: Between Novice and Expert—Living English, Moving Literacies   108

Epilogue: Stories as *Sangīnī*   119
A Brief Essay on Methods   121
Notes   127
Works Cited and Consulted   135
Index   143
Author   153

ACKNOWLEDGMENTS

THIS WORK WOULD NOT HAVE BEEN possible outside of collaborations with the language teachers, translators, field officers, facilitators, and learners of the Caritas Nepal Bhutanese Refugee Education Program in Kathmandu and Damak, Nepal. I am especially grateful to the following individuals: Sylvia Rai, Krishna Bir Magar, Sancha Subba, Amashi Urav, Yam Prasad Mainali, Parbati Khadka, Nima Dolma Sherpa, Pahalman Darjee, Kamali Adhikari, Indira Bhattarai, Thalu Niroula, Bishnu Rai, Dilu Rai, Pabitra Gazmer, Shyam Rani Tamang, and Tika Dungel; also the Reverend Fathers Pius Perumana; P. S. Amalraj, SJ; and Amritharaj.

Thank you to the resettled families who supported this project in its earliest formative stages, especially the Bhattarais, including Indira, Kamal, Ram, Niru, Mon Maya, and Narad, the Upretis, including Ram and Pampha, and Abi, Mamta, and their three children; and to the teachers, project managers, and community leaders who collaborated on this project in its post-resettlement contexts, including Masha Gromyko of the Pima Community College Refugee Education Project; Erina Delic of the Tucson International Alliance of Refugee Communities; Meg Fabry of Horizons for Refugee Families, Tucson; and Purna Budhathoki of the Bhutanese Mutual Assistance Association of Tucson.

Thank you to my sisters in spirit throughout India and Nepal, especially Sister Lourdu Mary, Sister Mary Kumari, Sister Nazarena, and the late Sister Amala for sharing many delicious meals and cups of tea, for your reading references and work notes, for the reverberations of your influence on my life—I am reminded of you when I invoke Kausila, "Cinnu bhayō, bōlnu bhayō, hāsnu bhayō, māyā sanga bhayō."; to Sister Mary, thank you for your prayers, for a friendship that is too deep for words, for nurturing my spirit, body, and mind while I lived so far from home.

To my academic friends, mentors, and community: to Anne Marie Hall for planting seeds by introducing me to comparative pedagogy, critical theory, and praxis, for your border-crossing work at the edge of the field, and for your encouragement; to Perry Gilmore for apprenticing me in the ethnography of literacy, but also in the art of serendipity, and the magic of evocation—*duende*; to Lauren Rosenberg, exceptional mentor, editor, friend: thank you for *The Desire for Literacy: Writing in the Lives of Adult Learners*, which inspires new, critical methods of listening to/(re)telling adult learner stories; to Amber Engelson, for your many close reads and theory-mindedness, for your *presence* and loving *fierceness*; to Roma Bhattarai, Atulya Acharya, Shekhar Rijal, Geeta Manandhar, and Steve Parks for your "word work"; to Steve, especially, for seeing potential in the messiest of drafts; to Stephanie Kerschbaum for moral support; to Cynthia Gomez at NCTE for your meticulous and timely shepherding of this project; to the IU Bloomington graduate students in my fieldwork and composition, literacy, and culture classes, thank you for your groundbreaking ideas, constructive criticism, and insightful commentary.

Many thanks to the various councils, conferences, symposia, forums, and research networks that have had a hand in bringing this work into its current form through workshops and presentation opportunities and through language and travel grants: to the South and Central Asia Fulbright Conference for bringing regional area studies researchers together to discuss our work; to the Indiana University Bloomington Arts and Humanities Council and the IU Office of the Vice President for International Affairs for travel and language learning grants; to the American Association of University Women Fellowship program; to the National Council of Teachers of English Annual Convention research strand and the Conference on College Composition and Communication Qualitative Research Network for early opportunities to present and receive feedback; to the American Anthropological Association Council on Anthropology and Education for works-in-progress forums and early-career mentoring; and to the organizers and participants of the 2016 University of Massachusetts Peter Elbow Symposium for the Study and Teaching of Writing on transnational literacies for your insightful comments and critical feedback.

I gratefully acknowledge financial support for this research from the Fulbright US Student Program, which is sponsored by the US Department of State, and the Commission for Educational Exchange between the United States and Nepal.[1]

To those associated with this work who must remain nameless due to our confidentiality agreements, thank you for your generosity, curiosity, and openheartedness in speaking with/to me.

PROLOGUE: *ANGRĒJĪ BHĀSĀ PADHNU BHANĒKŌ YASTAI HŌ!* / "LEARNING THE ENGLISH LANGUAGE IS LIKE THAT!": SUSMITA

"*BUDDHI ĀUNDAINA!* WISDOM DOESN'T COME!" Susmita leans way back from her seated position on the wooden bench at the instructors' worktable in the Beldangi I Bhutanese Refugee Camp Spoken English Center.

Moving her body forward over the table, she points to her forehead and laughs, "*Mērō dimāg gayō!* My brain is gone!"

"Education is important," she continues in Nepali, "but what can I do about it? It is the time for us to die, though I'm interested to learn. If I had studied earlier . . ." she trails off, then adds, "but I didn't know at that time."

Sitting across from one another, we are cobbling together conversation between my simplified Nepali and Susmita's colloquial blending of Nepali and Hindi. I'm a novice, and my Nepali is stilted, difficult to get out. I extend exasperated, sidelong glances at Susmita's English teacher, Parbati, a woman in her late twenties who grew up in the camps. Parbati sits unobtrusively at the far end of the table, intervening gently on my behalf when my language skills fail, which is often. Later, Susmita will point out to me the ways in which we are both tongued-tied, but not equivalently so. I'm white and speak English. I struggle with the basic spoken Nepali I learned from students in my adult literacy classes back home in Tucson and from a two-week language immersion program I completed in Kathmandu.

I've relied upon the intersections of my language, gender, race, class, and location to advance my educational agenda in ways that are nothing like Susmita's experience of language, literacy, and learning. I've chosen to learn Nepali, and feeling isolated at times, misunderstood, I struggle to twist my tongue around the nasal vowels and aspirated bilabials that my mouth and breath and vocal cords aren't used to making. At other times, I feel empowered by my new language skills, which allow me to meet my survival needs on a basic level, and even converse minimally, awkwardly, with acquaintances and the learners at the Spoken English Centers.

My struggle with language is amusing to Susmita and her friends, who, after several months of my daily visits, begin to refer to me using the endearingly diminutive relational term, *hāmro sānō bahini*, "our little sister."

"How come our little sister doesn't know Nepali yet?" I heard them whispering one day after a youthful Fulbright student from the United States visited Susmita's language center during an afternoon class and gave an uplifting speech about hard work and resilience. It was delivered in the most beautiful Nepali accent, eliciting much applause from the stunned and fascinated audience. The visitor came and went. Comparisons were made. I was embarrassed as I continued to struggle day in and day out with the language. Susmita struggled too, with English, but not in the same way that I struggled to learn Nepali.

While literacy in my first language, English, came to me early on in the context of a working-class parochial-school education in the US mid-Atlantic region, Susmita is pursuing "survival" literacies in English in the context of a refugee camp adult learning center administered by Jesuits from India. She has never been to school, and though she speaks Nepali fluently and can understand and use some Hindi loan words, she struggles to sign her name to important documents and to read notices posted by resettlement agencies in both Nepali and English.

As she speaks to me, Susmita wears a colorful woven blouse cinched at the waist by a thick band. A round, richly etched ornament about the size of a dime and the color of rich buttery gold adorns the side of her left nostril. Susmita's dress instantly identifies her as Indigenous Rai, a subgroup of one of the earliest inhabitants of eastern Nepal, the Kirat, and one of the largest Tibetan-Nepalese ethnic groups living throughout Nepal, India, and Bhutan. But I do not think to ask her about the Rai language. Did she also speak Rai at home? My limited focus on just two languages, Nepali and English, clouded my judgement, prevented me from considering more complicated multilingual contexts. And this, too, sets me and Susmita apart from one another.

Susmita and I also differ in age by almost twenty years. I'm thirty-three. The first few feathery smile lines are beginning to appear at the corners of my eyes, and day after day, I notice more and more gray hairs spread throughout the crown of my head (much to the distress of my Nepali host sisters, who beg me to try, at least, a little *amla*, a henna product, to cover them up). Susmita is fifty-two. Her skin, like that of other Rai women her age living in the camps, is browned and leathery from years of exposure; deep lines groove across her forehead and fan out from the corners of her eyes as she laughs. Her hair is dyed dark reddish brown, nearly black. Not a single gray hair in sight. Susmita has birthed children, watched them grow up in the rice fields in southern Bhutan and in the jungle of the refugee camps in Nepal. She worries about the future of her grandchildren, whom she describes as living with one foot in refugee life and one foot in village life; their mother, a local woman, lives outside of the camps.

Growing into adulthood in Bhutan, Susmita married young, cultivated rice fields, and never went to school. Now, she wants to learn English and is interested in resettlement but is not sure what the future holds. In the meantime, learning English is not easy. As soon as she learns a word, she forgets it, and then has to start all over again. Day in and day out, it is like this. Learning and forgetting. Studying for months on end and making little progress.

"After we reached here from Bhutan," Susmita says to me in Nepali, "we should have studied in Oxfam, but I didn't get a chance to read at that time because my children were very small. I didn't get time to go to school, and now I'm regretting it a lot.

"But what can I do? I am getting old. My brain is gone! I am coming and going from school and forgetting words that were just said! Doing such things, going to school, I hope that I may remember. Now I can write my name a bit and make a signature, but I have only learned that much education here. Before, I did not know how to write my name. Now I can, and I'm happy with that."

Susmita is but one woman among thousands, displaced here, in the Nepali Terai, a region blanketed by jungle and rich, wet alluvial plains that run the length of Nepal's southeasternmost border with India. Living out her adult life in a refugee camp, surrendering daily to the vicissitudes of an ongoing resettlement process, Susmita arrives to English class each morning with an NGO-issued blue notebook and pencil. She practices drawing lines and making curves. She recites: A, B, C. She sits cross-legged on a woven mat in a bamboo hut among a couple of dozen women, ages twenty-five to seventy, diverse in their ethnolinguistic and religious backgrounds and resettlement status.

They say, "*English is for everything!*"

"*We must learn!*"

"*Our daughters call us from over there and say, please learn and then come quickly!*"

They give reasons for learning English that seem to reinforce the larger narrative that English is for "everything," for maintaining connections and making progress, for surviving a seemingly never-ending resettlement process and bringing an end to their protracted displacement.

But there are other reasons, too.

As Kausila, a woman featured later in this book, puts it, "*Cinnu bhayō, bōlnu bhayō, hāsnu bhayō! Māyā sanga bhayō*"—"One advantage of our learning together is that we got to know each other, we spoke and laughed. It happened with love." Women come alive to one another in and through their learning. They become *moved* to know, speak, laugh and love together in solidarity, despite their differences.

This book attends to the stories of five women—Susmita, Suk Maya, Kali Maya, Abi Maya, and Kausila—caught between the "here" and "there," the "before" and "after" of an ongoing refugee resettlement process. They are around Susmita's age and have been living in refugee camps tucked away, deep inside Nepal's southern jungles, for nearly a quarter of a century. My narrative encounters with these women took place primarily from 2012 to 2013, at the midpoint of a massive Bhutanese refugee resettlement program administered by the United Nations High Commissioner for Refugees (UNHCR), the International Organization for Migration

(IOM), and national governments. Most of the women in this book are learning to read and write in English as a language of expediency tied to their impending resettlements to English-speaking countries. Many of these women have very little to no prior education in literacy and are developing literacy in a language other than their first. Coming together at language centers created and sustained by refugee women, like Parbati, who are half their age and educated within the camps' system of English-medium secondary schools, these older women struggle with the effects of aging and generational differences that characterize the possibilities and constraints of their desire to learn.

Alongside women's stories of experience, I engage in a series of self-reflexive ethnographic narratives in the form of snapshots and time lapses that move back and forth in time across sites of learning. In the snapshots and timelapses of my ethnographic narrative encounters with women learning English in diaspora, I become what the feminist ethnographer Ruth Behar has called the "vulnerable observer." This observer is no longer hidden behind the mask of authority of a disembodied, omniscient narrator, but called into ethnical relationship with and by the women who tell their stories. This observer is an embodied listener/teller, invited into acts of translation that are risky for everyone involved, but not equally so. After my encounters with these women, I go home, back to teaching and writing, back to family and friends. Whereas everyday life for Susmita and her peers is precarious, home is an unstable construct, family and friends have been scattered across the globe, the future remains uncertain and unsettled. Their experiences of storied knowledge are different from mine. But together our stories work as part of a relational and dialogic methodology for translating the textured and dynamic rhetoricity of women's narrativized experiences of learning across borders.

Working across stories, others' stories as well as my own, is an exercise in listening/(re)telling that responds to Eleanor Cushman, Damián Baca, and Romeo García's call for a storied research praxis that draws from "multiple streams of evidence and loci of enunciation" (14). In another sense, this book is an experiment in re-presenting storied knowledge not as "evidence" of transnational realities but as a form of coperformative inquiry. It proposes a new kind of literacy research in the context of global (im)mobilities that is less about the discursive representation of literate events and practices mirroring translocal realities than it is about the situated layers of the interpretative meaning-making that people engage in across their differences to evoke, enact, and affect literate action and meanings.

Throughout the book, I refer to the stories here as *living-English stories* after the rhetoric and composition scholar Min-Zhan Lu's term "living-English work," which Lu describes as an effort to make a language such as English "'carry' the burden of . . . particular lived experience[s] . . . [and] relations" (609). Living-English stories are stories of English language and literacy learning drawn from "lived experience," yet they are not meant to mirror or reflect the transnational realities of events and practices. Rather, I understand them as situated layers in the interpretive framing of events and practices that animate the valuing of literacies in transnational motion. In this way, this book approaches listening to and (re)telling stories about language, literacy, and learning as collaboratively grounded, embodied, and mutable coperformances that emerge in constellated relation to others. This book does not offer an "analysis" of women, or their literacies, as the subject of its research as much as it does an exploration of thinking with, "speaking nearby" and "speaking with and to" women's accounts of language, literacy, and learning (Trinh 101; see also Chen 86–87; Alcoff 23). As such, it seeks to trouble the divide between storied experiences and disciplinary framings of transnational literacy learning, cocreating, alongside women's stories, a performative, moving research praxis that attempts the "impossible" (Spivak "Afterword"), an ethical navigating of the space between story and theory that reaches beyond learning as an act of accumulating resources to something more akin to flourishing together.

Living English, Moving Literacies is a dialogic performance of speaking with/to others' stories about the possibilities and constraints of learning English. It is a lively assemblage of enunciations and negotiations, situated in the context of a protracted, ongoing displacement and refugee resettlement process. It brings the local, the embodied, and the mutable to bear on questions of literacy and mobility within the field of rhetoric and writing studies in order to rethink literacy as both a cultural practice and a means of creating and maintaining translocal ties. What isn't this book? It isn't a book for people seeking a how-to manual on partnering with refugees, extracting their stories, or better understanding their plight in relationship to the development of writing skills or acquisition of alphabetic literacies for economic accumulations, as it doesn't offer a sense that literacy matters in this way, at least not to the women featured here. Nor does it provide any definitive answers or frameworks for accomplishing literacy outcomes tied to survival or progress. Instead, what is offered here is a weighing of the hope and violence of English, a sharing of stories and introspections, a consideration of the effects of contamination and complicity, and an active reworking of our literacy myths. Here, I put into practice what "learning to learn" means in relation to cultivating responsibility *to*, rather than *for*, others (Spivak "Afterword" 200; "Responsibility"). The moving literacies indexed by women's living-English stories exceed the theoretical boundaries of literacy events and practices, trouble triumphant literacy narratives, and contribute to a critical reorientation to transnational literacy learning. These are not narratives of accommodation or resistance. These women's living-English stories, instead, offer to those who dare to listen, coming and going, and body to body, other possibilities, other openings for receiving and experiencing the gifts and challenges of our living, breathing, pulsing encounters with difference.

But first it is important to note the way the story of this research came to intersect with women's stories of experience and how this all came about in the middle of things, at the midpoint of a massive, decade-long resettlement process, and in the transnational space between the before and after of a complicated, protracted displacement. In the following pages, I provide some brief context for storytelling, for approaching moving literacies beyond a theory of accumulation, and for an ethics of speaking with/to.

INTRODUCTION
STARTING PLACES: LANGUAGE AND LITERACY LEARNING BETWEEN PRE- AND POST-RESETTLEMENT CONTEXTS

Introduction

Starting Places: Language and Literacy Learning between Pre- and Post-Resettlement Contexts

THE STORY OF HOW I CAME TO BE INVOLVED in the resettlement of Bhutanese refugees began in 2008. I was working toward my Adult Basic Education (ABE) teaching certification in Arizona and volunteering at the Pima County Community College Adult Education Refugee Education Project, a grant-funded language and literacy training program for adult refugee arrivals within their first five years of resettlement. For the next seven years, I taught courses to adult learners of refugee status from all over the world. By 2010, however, I began to notice a distinct shift in classroom demographics. This was about two years after the start of the Bhutanese refugee resettlement program in the United States and fewer and fewer students were coming from African and Middle Eastern countries. For a time, from about 2010 to 2013, my classes mainly comprised older, Nepali-speaking women, ranging in age from mid-twenties to seventy. These women were deeply invested in learning to read, write, and speak English, though few would progress beyond perfunctory greetings. Still, many of these women devoted years of their lives to daily coursework in the program. Indeed, it was these women's years-long investments in developmental English programs, their persistence and refusal to quit, despite not making the measurable gains in proficiency that would satisfy economically driven program outcomes, that prompted me to begin asking the questions and listening to the stories that would eventually lead to this book.

In 2015, I joined a community working group of language and literacy educators in partnership with a statewide language policy and planning initiative organized by Arizona's Department of Economic Security and the US Office of Refugee Resettlement. Our working group was tasked with assessing community needs for language and literacy training in dialogue with local voluntary agencies (VOLAGs), mutual assistance associations, and other community groups. As an adult educator collaborating at the local level with these community partners, I found questions of how best to implement language support for recent immigrant arrivals, and to what effect, looming large. Certainly, language and literacy acquisition for older adults with little to no formal educational experience, and women, especially, had been a top priority of the mutual assistance associations led by refugee community leaders. In conversations with the president-elect of the Bhutanese Mutual Assistance Association of Tucson (BMAAT), for example, I came to learn that women's education in English, along with eldercare, language maintenance, and cultural education, were BMAAT's primary goals. In fact, these goals had been written into the mission statement of the organization by community members as part of their application for 501(c)(3) (nonprofit) status. Still, my interviews with women attending the free English classes being offered by various volunteer agencies across the city revealed narratives about literacy learning that equivocated about its usefulness, investments in learning that reflected partial and complicated commitments to language acquisition, and deeper histories of language use, attainment, and denial than had been relayed to me in meetings and conversations with community-based organizational leadership. It seemed that women were living out investments in English differently from programmatic and organizational mandates and discourses. Their moving literacies, and related commitments and practices of learning, told another story.

Meanwhile, as the students in my Saturday morning ESL classes gradually become aware of my interest in women's literacy in the Bhutanese refugee camps, they helped connect me to camp leaders and teachers with whom I might talk and exchange resources. Then, one Saturday morning after class, with the help of a student and her husband, I made a call to the office assistant of the field director of Caritas Nepal's Bhutanese Refugee Education Program, the nongovernmental agency responsible for implementing grassroots educational initiatives in the camps. Through the grainy static of the long-distance call, I introduced myself and a nascent idea, a year-long collaboration and research project involving class visits, interviews, and document collection among adult English language learners and facilitators across our programs. Following a series of email communications lasting nearly six months, I was sent a letter of affiliation in support of my proposed plan. I arrived in Nepal in late July 2012 as a Fulbright student and researcher in rhetoric, composition, and the teaching of English with a focus on literacy education.

I spent roughly ten months living and working in Nepal, from August 2012 to June 2013. For most of that time, I worked as a Caritas Nepal volunteer, teaching English in the camps and assisting the Spoken English Center resource teachers. I led trainings and workshops, attended instructional meetings, and spoke with hundreds of adult learners. When it was time to leave, I had accumulated a digital hard drive full of stories, snapshots, and reflections that I promised the learners and resource teachers of the Spoken English Centers I would share with educators back home. Yet as I began to share these materials at conferences and in working groups, I struggled to find a way to frame them for US-based educators. The focus in language training for recently resettled refugees at that time was vocational training and self-sufficiency. Educational gains were documented as time-to-employability even though the women's stories that I had collected ran counter to these economic goals. It was difficult to try and make sense of women's stories for other educators outside of an economy of upward mobility and personal advancement. What use were these traveling stories if they did not produce the literate outcomes necessary for economic solvency?

BEYOND ACCUMULATION: LANGUAGES, LITERACIES, AND LEARNING IN MOTION

Within the field of rhetoric and composition, transnational language and literacy practices have often been framed within economies of mobility. Such economies have been filled with discussions of the development of writing in migrant communities, the complexity of individual and community-based multilingual resources, the need for textual mobilities, and the ways literacy encounters social-material forces. As a result, how we imagine literacy in motion has been profoundly influenced by a concept of an economy of literacy moving through global markets and involving deep histories of sponsorship that both afford and constrain literacy's mobility. The question of literacies' mobility, first posed by Deborah Brandt in introducing the conceptual apparatus of literacy sponsorship, is still relevant. It helps to re-frame our understanding of literacy resources and investments in an economic sense, spurring questions of how the material stuff of literacy as capital is embedded within contexts of individual literacy development.

Similarly, Brandt's notion of "accumulating literacy," of writing resources "piling up and extending out of literacy and its technologies," stems from a theory of capital accumulation (Brandt, "Accumulating Literacy," 651). Interested in the effects of accumulating literacies and their implications for writing research, Brandt explores "how the proliferation of print affects the occasions and motivations for learning to read and write" (653), as well as what people do with writing resources in economies of literacy that value accumulation and amalgamation. She finds that "new reading and writing practices" are constituted "in response to rapid social change" (651). The central question for Brandt is "[h]ow are we (in rhetoric and writing studies) to understand the vicissitudes of individual literacy development in relationship to large-scale economic forces that set the routes and determine the worldly worth of that literacy?" ("Sponsors" 166).

Yet, as Iswari P. Pandey has discussed, it's "tricky" to talk about what is called "literacy in motion" or the "migrantness of literacy," because of the autonomous and decontextualized view of literacy skills often read into such concepts (22–23). A concept of literacy as sets of practices in motion is also limited, argues Pandey, in that it fails to consider the ways in which literate activity is involved in creating, maintaining, mediating, and negotiating social relations in and across local and translocal contexts. Pandey suggests a view of literacy as word and symbol work—"word work"—that is always in motion, "unsettled and unsettling" entanglements of value, identity, and agency (26). Tied to Brandt's concept of literacy sponsorship, Pandey's idea of the migrantness of literacy describes the way immigrant communities commit to and draw possibilities for literacy out of the wake of state and corporate sponsorships that leave them behind. Pandey argues that the word work that defines migrant community literacies in motion "is not work in the economic sense of return but cultural capital that yields value in the form of recognition and status" and "involves real work in terms of time, energy, and resources" (29).

Further complicating the discourse of literacy, mobility, and agency in immigrant communities, the works of Rebecca Lorimer Leonard and Kate Vieira examine the products and processes of literacies in motion. Leonard in her work on migrant women and writing resources "on the move" seeks to understand mobility in terms of inequalities defined by "choice." Leonard writes, "Having the choice to move or to stay put, to mobilize oneself or one's literacies, is a form of economically and socially advantageous control" (*Writing* 10). Her project is one of investigating different qualities of literate movements—fluid, fixed, and frictive—and what these kinds of mobility mean for the value of literacy, especially writing, in the everyday lives of highly literate, multilingual migrant women.

Vieira argues for a sociomaterial theory of migrant literacy that depends on an "accumulation of associations not with assimilation but authority, legitimacy, and mobility" (*American by Paper* 142). Literacy is "a mobile complex of practices and products, installed with meaning both by institutions and by the people under their thrall" (142). This is the "interplay between process and product" that defines the relationship between literacy and mobility for

Vieira (142). But Vieira also cautions us that literacy access does not necessarily equal full agency, as migrants' control of literacy products and processes is "only as strong as the strongest of them" (qtd. in Leonard, *Writing on the Move*, 12).

However, as I came to know refugee-background, adult learners, like Susmita in Nepal, my perspective on transnational literacy learning began to shift away from a US-centric focus on the accumulation of multilingual resources for movement. Instead, I began to see Susmita's transnational literacies, and that of her peers, in terms of an ongoing effort to reconstruct and reconstitute their lives in displacement. They approach language and literacy learning as one creative response to the tensions of local and global forces shaping an uncertain future. Susmita and many of her peers were less concerned with becoming proficient in English than they were with forming solidarity with other women who also attended classes, and through their daily learning practice they found a supportive community for living with and through the challenges of resettlement.

What if Susmita's aim in learning English wasn't as she said, to become literate for refugee resettlement, but was in the service of another knowledge-making practice? Or what if Susmita's desire for literacy in motion was both an effort to learn for migration purposes as well as in defiance of a life spent without access to education, a way through the tensions and contradictions of living in protracted displacement? What if in her narrative encounters with me, instead of evidencing the (im)mobilities of particular sets of literacy resources, Susmita is re-narrating and re-forming the very notion of literacy itself in response to the tensions of resettlement, including its imperative that refugees should act like migrating workers, taking up English for their survival and self-sufficiency? What if Susmita's desire to become literate isn't motivated by accumulating literacy resources for personal and economic advancement as much as a desire to engage in some other kind of critical work?

Scholars of transnational literacies in the field of rhetoric and composition have contributed important thinking to the relationship between people's investments in literacy and economies of literacy as part of the production of literacy hope. They make a defensible argument for why and how certain kinds of literacy matter to precarious individuals within an economy of accumulation. But when Western concepts of social field and capital are used to determine how people value literacy, it becomes difficult to hear the cultural production of meaning beyond capital accumulation. What if, as Susmita intimates, transnational literacy is not just synonymous with resources, fluency, and choice, but with gendered, corporeal, and collective experiences of uneven access to educational resources and opportunities that are contoured by forced transnational movements and volatility? What if a different sense of agency, ambivalence, and (im)mobility is in play?

As I got to know Susmita in the refugee camps, she expressed uncertainty about the future and ambivalence about learning English at her age. In 2012, Bhutanese refugee resettlement was at its midpoint. Hundreds of people were leaving the camp each week, boarding charter buses for the IOM's resettlement processing compound in Kathmandu, and then traveling onward to countries of resettlement, mostly the United States, but also Australia, Canada, the United Kingdom, and Belgium. Teachers and learners at the Spoken English Centers left the camps almost as soon as I could interview them. Yet the camps I visited, three at the time—Beldangi I, Beldangi II, and Sanischare—felt full, choked to capacity. In fact, the camps were very much alive with bustling markets, crowded thoroughfares, and packed primary and secondary schools. The energy in the air was electric. There was much anticipation and anxiety about the future. What would happen to the people who refused to resettle? Would the donor agencies that had been supporting them for nearly two decades continue to do so? What would integration into local communities look like and mean? Of the people going for resettlement, what would life be like in yet a third country? Would they find jobs and be able to feed themselves and their families? What would it be like to practice their religious beliefs and customs outside of Nepal? Some members of the older generations, especially, refused to leave Nepal out of concern for what would become of their burial rites and fear of what would happen to their bodies when they died. Would God recognize them on the other side of the globe?

Susmita was among over twenty-five thousand people displaced from Bhutan living in the camps when I visited in 2012–2013, a number down from nearly ninety thousand people who were already resettled. Susmita, like many of the Bhutanese refugees in Nepal, would trace her ancestry back through generations of indigenous peoples from the eastern, hilly regions of Nepal who migrated into southern Bhutan in the late 1800s. They were part of a larger eastward movement of agrarian laborers of various ethnolinguistic and religious groups who sought to escape the destitute conditions of subsistence farming and exploitation of the peasantry during the reign of the Gorkhalis in Nepal. They were permitted to cultivate land in southern Bhutan and were loosely administered by regional officers.

It was not until 1958, however, that the southern Bhutanese of Nepali origin were granted citizenship rights under Bhutan's first ordinance on matters of nationality, the Nationality Law of 1958. Under this ordinance, citizenship was granted to foreigners who petitioned appointed officials and declared their loyalty to the monarchy. Citizenship would be granted if it were recognized that the petitioner was of the age to naturalize and had lived in Bhutan for ten or more years. In that way, Nepalis living in southern Bhutan who met these conditions of citizenship came to be recognized by the Bhutanese government as subjects of Bhutan (Hutt 134).

Susmita came of age in Bhutan at a time when schools were opened, roads were built, and policies were implemented that promoted the integration of Nepali-speaking Bhutanese citizens into the social fabric of Bhutan. But beginning in the late 1970s, these integration efforts began to slow. A new Citizenship Act of 1977 revised requirements for citizenship, lengthening the period of residency at the time of petition to a minimum of twenty years instead of ten and requiring some knowledge of Dzongkha, the national language of Bhutan (Hutt 147). The new citizenship requirements also made it more challenging for the foreign-born spouses of Bhutanese nationals to apply for citizenship, an amendment to the original law made in an attempt to curtail the common practice of bringing wives from India and Nepal across the border into Bhutan (149). Further restrictions to naturalization were imposed under the 1988 census, which was carried out to identify foreigners and issue citizenship identity cards to true Bhutanese nationals. In order to qualify for the census, individuals needed to produce a tax receipt dated 1958, the year in which the first Nationality Law was enacted. Additionally, if the individual resided in a block or district different from the place of origin at the time of the 1958 Nationality Law, the individual needed to produce a CO, or certificate of origin. For the census, individuals were added to one of seven lists based on their ability to procure the required documents (153). The lists described citizenship eligibility and the status of one's nationality along the following lines:

> F1 Genuine Bhutanese citizens
> F2 Returned migrants (people who had left Bhutan and then returned)
> F3 "Drop-out" cases—i.e., people who were not around at the time of the census
> F4 A non-national woman married to a Bhutanese man
> F5 A non-national man married to a Bhutanese woman
> F6 Adoption cases (children who have been legally adopted)
> F7 Non-nationals, i.e., migrants and illegal settlers (*Bhutan* 5)

Early on, few of the Nepali-speaking Bhutanese were categorized as F7. In later stages of the 1988 census, however, individuals' status fluctuated, and census operations began against suspected dissidents and their families (Hutt 156). Political tension grew as new policies related to culture, national dress, and language were introduced.

In late 1990, a series of demonstrations organized by resistance parties swept across southern Bhutan. Following the demonstrations, the Bhutanese army and police began identifying participants and supporters, arresting them, and holding them without trial for several months. Many of these prisoners were released by amnesties of the king under the condition that they would leave Bhutan with their families. Census takers then returned to villages, reclassifying individuals with ties to prisoners under different census categories. Many of the Nepali-speaking Bhutanese left Bhutan at this time under duress from the Bhutanese army and local officials. A program of "voluntary emigration" enacted by Bhutanese officials in the area saw a mass exodus from Bhutan's southern districts, mainly individuals and families with ties to India and Nepal who, under this duress, filed forms requesting permission to emigrate to Nepal, at the same time forfeiting identification papers and land rights to the government.

The first Nepali-speaking Bhutanese entered Nepal through the district of Jhapa at the end of 1990 (see QR code). In September 1991, the government of Nepal requested the assistance of the UNHCR to coordinate emergency aid assistance, and by 1994 seven camps had been established in Jhapa and Morang districts (see QR code). Six years later, over ninety thousand people were registered in the camps, including a growing number of children (Hutt 258). After decades of failed talks among governmental and nongovernmental agencies, it was clear that neither repatriation to Bhutan nor integration in Nepal would be a viable option for the Bhutanese refugees. Thus, an extraordinarily complex process of refugee resettlement commenced that would continue for yet another decade.

Trapped by Inequality: Bhutanese Refugee Women in Nepal

Susmita was just twenty-eight years old when she was forced to leave Bhutan with her family. By the time we met, she had been living in the camps for over two decades. She had lived through the failed attempts at repatriation and the gradual shift to resettlement. As with many displaced people the world over, questions of identity, tradition, national belonging, and community hung heavy over Susmita's life in the camps, and her future was far from certain.

During resettlement, Susmita vacillated between excitement at the thought of leaving the camps and uncertainty about what life would be like post-resettlement. There were problems with her case, and she had not yet received a date from the IOM for leaving the camps. Susmita was distraught about this and was taking English classes to pass the time during this indefinite period of waiting. Women referred to this time between the start of a resettlement process and leaving the camps as "date waiting," and it could be excruciating. At the midpoint of resettlement, date waiting was a common state of liminal temporality for many people still living in the camps. The unproblematic cases, the ones whose asylum narratives and circumstances fit the measures of legitimacy defined by the UNCHR, had already been processed and left the camps. That left the more complicated cases to pile up, sometimes for years. Indeed, nearly everyone I spoke with in 2012 and 2013 had a problem with their case that had led to weeks and months, if not years, of date waiting. Susmita was no exception.

In the meantime, Susmita attended English classes at Caritas Nepal's Spoken English Centers among other women close in age. Many of these women, like Susmita, grew up in the rural southern lowlands of Bhutan's swampy forests as agrarian laborers. Many women self-identified as either a *khetālo* (farm laborer) or a *go Thālo* (herder). In Bhutan, lack of proximity to formal schools as well as gendered practices related to domestic work, agrarian life, and family roles limited women's access to primary education. Most women attending classes at the language centers in the camps had never been to school and could not read or write in any language, while a younger generation of women came of age of age speaking and writing in English in the camp's English-medium primary and secondary schools. Despite this uneven access to literate resources compared with younger generations of women living in the camps, the women who came to learn at the language centers often committed themselves to months or years of learning during the resettlement period, despite making little progress in their oral fluency or written proficiency.

There was, according to Susmita and her peers at the Spoken English Centers, *sukha-dukha*, happiness as well as hardship to be found in learning to read and write for the first time in English as the language of resettlement. Many of the learners in the Spoken English Centers were considered by their communities to be too old to learn. In coming to the centers, they were forced to fight against larger cultural assumptions that older women had no place in school. Yet now they finally had the opportunity to learn. Learning was a joyful gift enabled by a powerful NGO and by young women teachers from within their own communities; it was one of the few advantages of being caught up in an interminable displacement.

The imbricated experiences of happiness and suffering that characterized women's learning and their investments in English worked at the edges of my study, gently coaxing me to consider not the ways in which women were taking hold of the mobile language resources at their disposal to become literate, but the way in which women, in their everyday stories and performances of learning, were challenging the very assumption that I held, along with others in my field of work and study, that they were learning *for the purposes of becoming more mobile*. Indeed, many women who spoke with me articulated their desire for other learning outcomes, where their increased mobility through migration would be possible regardless of whether or not they learned to read or write. Instead, women sought survival literacy skills, to be able to know and recognize letters and signage, to read and write their names and the names of their children, while engaging in other forms of connection through their learning beyond the accumulation of language resources for personal advancement, including gaining familiarity with other women in sensuous collaborations and solidarity: singing and dancing, talking and laughing, together, learning with love.

Extending out from Susmita's story and Pandey's critique of literacy and mobility, I understand literacy as the capacity, not just to amalgamate new reading and writing practices proffered by capitalist sponsors out of motives of profit-making and competition, but to sense, feel, and know—or to experience—through the active negotiation of *the hope and violence of literacy* what it means to take up literate resources for other, purposeful ends (Branch "Literacy Hope"). In framing women's stories as living-English stories, I am engaging with women as learners *and* as language users and agents, negotiating a creative response to the hope of literacy and the denial of literacy (literacy violence) through their stories of experience and everyday performances of literacy learning. In this way, the women of this book upend the conceptual apparatus of sponsorship embedded in economies of literacy tied to progress and, in doing so, recast our theoretical frameworks and research paradigms of transnational literacies. In this book, they do this through experience-oriented, living-English stories, stories *about* English language learning that refract the ambiguities, contradictions, betrayals, and deep, visceral longings of lived experience. They offer realms of possibility rooted in physical, face-to-face encounters across difference. This book structures living-English stories not as "heart-to-heart" confidences but as examples of the "tête-à-tête," critically intimate conversations among listeners and tellers, and as "performances of possibility," that help to expand and complicate each other's worlds and framings of language and literacy learning on the move and in contexts of border crossings and forced migration.[1]

SPEAKING WITH/TO: STORYTELLING AS A "PERFORMANCE OF POSSIBILITIES" ACROSS LANGUAGES, LOCATIONS, AND TIME

Listening to and (re)telling women's stories of learning has helped me to consider the ways in which the easy transnational promises of English language training programs mask more difficult dynamics. Storytelling through multi-sited narrative ethnography, through the re-presentation in research writing of intersecting stories of experience, reveals the complexity of literacy practices in the transnational contexts of women's (im)mobilities but also raises questions about the ethics of representation and the claims made by storytellers. Living-English stories matter for these reasons. Working with stories, not as evidence for literacies on the move, but as creative responses to "literacy hope" and to "the violence of literacy," opens a realm of possibility for speaking with/to others across difference that is coconstructed, dialogic, performative, articulated, contingent, and ethical.

Part of the ethics of such encounters involves claims to ownership and the right to (re)tell stories, which rest on the degree to which either party considers their narrative encounters to be like a living contract that adapts to change.[2] If my encounter with Susmita is read not as a static description of an interview process that indexes a set of shifting literate values that I extract for research purposes but as an active negotiation, then our story becomes a living story, grounded and mutable, not a dead artifact that I've packaged in theory. I encourage readers of this book to engage the stories here as a discursive negotiation of literate histories, experiences, and desires that intersect at the local crossroads of global flows and (im)mobilities—my own and others'. Indeed, our encounters weigh dominant discourses of what English can do for people in and out of resettlement against individual histories of both access and denial. Women weigh the promises of learning English against the corporeal and cultural constraints of aging that limit what and how they learn. In their stories about coming and going from the Spoken English Centers, they allude to what they must navigate, the complex assemblage of possibility and constraint that is English in a global context (Leonard, *Writing*). In speaking with and to me about their experiences of learning, women engage with me in ongoing, transactional "word work" (Pandey *South Asian*; Lu "Living-English Work"). Though we may speak in "broken" forms of Nepali and English, we artfully and collectively draw on our emergent language resources not to move past one another in our pursuit of border crossings but to connect across our lived difference, to "limn" lived experience, to use what language we have to "make sense of" and "shape" relationality between ourselves and the enterprise of global English learning (Lu "Living-English Work"). This translingual and living-English work is a kind of speaking with/to, a "shared responsibility" that we set apart from the extractive, exploitative work of an ethnography that theory-builds on the backs of other people's stories.

In the field of writing and rhetoric studies, there are other scholar-researchers who work in story with adult learners. This book contributes to an ongoing conversation. For cases in point, both Tika Lamsal and Lauren Rosenberg in their book-length studies of adult literacy in informal, community literacy contexts participate in new forms of ethics-centered, noncoercive listening/(re)telling that prioritize "word work" and relationship. In *Globalizing Literacies and Identities: Translingual and Transcultural Literacy Practices of Bhutanese Refugees in the US*, Lamsal offers a rich ethnographic and community-centered analysis of generational literacy practices across languages in post-resettlement contexts. Drawing from translation scholarship that discusses the practice of "literal translation" as a negotiated process of meaning-making that is sensitive to political, social, and cultural histories, Lamsal argues for ethnographic research in rhetoric and composition that carefully considers researcher-participant relationships, insider-outsider positionality, and representational ethics through transparent descriptions of translation processes.

Similarly, in *The Desire for Literacy: Writing in the Lives of Adult Learners*, Rosenberg (re)presents the dialogue between the researcher and participants as a form of rhetorical listening that is constantly negotiating the means and meanings of intent on the part of the researcher-as-listener versus author. Troubling their own identifications and unconscious biases as researcher-writer-translators in relation to their participants and subjects of study, Lamsal and Rosenberg encourage new forms of narrative encounter that break open the sedimentation of "experience-distant terms" that has characterized much of the more empirical research on writing and literacy in the field so far. They also argue for narrative methods as collaboration between researchers and participants across languages and literacies in translingual and transcultural contexts

(Lamsal) as well as across individual histories and experiences of literacy development in the context of adult learning (Rosenberg).

As a listener/storyteller who did not share the same degree of language proficiency or pragmatic knowledge of spoken and written forms of Nepali as participants, I worked with many translators and interpreters throughout my time teaching English and documenting stories in the United States and Nepal. Reflecting critically on these collaborations, I have considered the value of the literal translation versus the performance of storytelling in English. In the end, I chose to work at the intersections of literal and more performative forms of translation and writing. The methodological choices I've made through my negotiated encounters with others speak to my own positionality, emergent plurilingual knowledge, and shifting power dynamics relative to others. My decision not to produce literal transcriptions of stories in Nepali alongside the English translation is a consequence of these intersections.

Rather than literal transcriptions and translations, I have tried in this book to work at the cusp between transnational "realities" and storytelling as a coperformance of (im)possibilities. Echoing Cushman, Baca, and García, I want to argue for the value of ethnographic narrative writing as a performance of polyphonic listening/telling that reroutes the "locus of enunciation of knowledge" from the author/ethnographer to "multiple loci for enunciating knowledge and multiple streams of evidence" (11–14). With them, I advocate for a move beyond self-centered storytelling as a *"trope for methods"* (11) to storytelling that can contribute to "pluriversal understandings" and story "as testimony and bearing witness," "as stemming from and contributing to Indigenous communities," and as "crucial to the work of self-reflexivity in ethnographies and case studies" (13).

Relatedly, Carmen Kynard and Bernadette M. Calafell promote intersectional reflexive storytelling in their pedagogical writings and situated and embodied disciplinary reflections. They announce a call for methods of portraiture (of learners and students) as costorytelling (Kynard) and the value of personal experience in theory-making (Calafell). Both shift the focus from text-centered paradigms to storytelling as a processual, embodied coperformance in contexts of intersectional difference and cross-boundary discourse. Quoting from Moraga and Anzaldúa, Calafell values personal experience in knowledge-making as "theory in the flesh," and seeks a *rhetorics of possibility* that fuses critical rhetorical perspectives with a politics of performance (106).

For both Kynard and Calafell, storytelling and performance offer a space of possibility to scholars of color in rhetorical studies who face challenges to their documentation of minority voices and who are all too acutely aware of the possibilities and impossibilities of working within and outside of disciplinary conventions and expectations, particularly when it comes to scholarly writing. In performance studies, and in D. Soyini Madison's critical ethnography work, Calafell finds echoes of Moraga and Anzaldúa's "theory in the flesh." Citing Madison, Calafell writes: "Performance helps me live a truth while theory helps me name it—or maybe it is the other way around . . . the theory knows and feels, and the performance feels and unlearns. I know I am a un/learning body in the process of feeling" (qtd. in "Rhetorics" 113). Through performance studies, Calafell bridges theories of the flesh to the work of the rhetorical scholar in "bringing critical attention to questions of voice, reflexivity, and agency" in "[o]ther types of texts and knowledge production" (115).

Performance scholar and critical ethnographer D. Soyini Madison uses the term "performance of possibilities" to discuss ethnography as a staged performance that involves subjects, audience members, and performers. Subjects are those whose experience is being performed in writing. Audiences are the readers of ethnographic writing and witnesses to the performance. And performers are the ethnographer/researcher/curators who costructure, compose, and enact the performance in dialogue with subjects and readers (190). It is worth quoting Madison at length here:

> In a performance of possibilities, the possible suggests a movement culminating in creation and change. It is the active, creative work that weaves the life of the mind with being mindful of life, of merging the text with the world, of

critically traversing the margin and center, and of opening more and different paths for enlivening relations and spaces. A performance of possibilities raises several questions for the ethnographer: By what definable and material means will subjects themselves benefit from the performance? How can the performance contribute to a more enlightened and involved citizenship that will disturb systems and processes that limit freedoms and possibilities? In what ways will the [performer] probe questions of identity, representation, and fairness to enrich their own subjectivity, cultural politics, and art? (191)

Conceiving of women's living-English stories as part of a performance and rhetoric of possibility demands the awareness that the author-performer's enactment of knowledge is always "partial, contingent, and relative" (Madison 196). Therefore, the author-performer does not attempt to speak for participants nor does the author-performer assume that they have the wherewithal to intervene on anyone's behalf. Yet at the same time, the performer-author must accept the responsibility of representation, "for the creation of what and who is being represented" (196).

In the performance of possibility this responsibility might take the form of what postcolonial feminist theorist and translator Gayatri Chakravorty Spivak has described as responsibility *to* versus *for* the subjects of the research. In the ethnography of literacy as a staged performance of possibilities, the researchers' responsibility is to the subjects of the performance, to the ways in which the subjects of the research have invited researchers into performance and dialogue where there is the "possibility of re-making" the relationship between researchers and researched (Madison 197). Spivak describes this as an invitation to ethical encounter, a call to read and write encounters differently, a call that must come from "below," meaning from a subaltern place and perspective, or from participants themselves.

Listening and (re)telling as coperformance and as a performance of possibility requires our critical attention to the notion that "literacy translations" can be transparent, that they can reveal what lies beneath descriptions of the initial narrative encounter, that translations can stand alone. As Linda Alcoff writes in "The Problem of Speaking for Others," certain kinds of listening/(re) telling are problematic insofar as they may promote listening to "oppressed" others who have less power than the listener without contextualization. Alcoff critiques the "self-abnegating intellectual" who listens to but "rejects speaking for others on the grounds that [they] can represent their own true interests" (22). This "retreat" by intellectuals into listening reinforces "a particular conception of experience (as transparent and self-knowing) . . . [that] essentializes [others] as nonideologically constructed subjects" (22). The antidote to this, according to Alcoff, is to "strive to create wherever possible the conditions for dialogue and the practice of *speaking with and to* rather than speaking for others" (23, my emphasis).³

Relatedly, Spivak writes about what it means "to learn to learn" from another's experience without appropriation as a lifelong commitment to the ethical (im)possibilities of dialogic translation: a singular (i.e., nonreplicable), processual renegotiation of the terms of relationship between oneself and others ("Afterword" 200). For me, learning to learn is an ongoing process of listening and (re)telling that continues beyond the immediacy of an initial dialogic and narrative encounter. Learning to learn is not knowledge extraction; it's an ongoing relational process of knowledge cocreation that entails a yielding to others' stories without self-abnegation. Yet it is important to be mindful that learning to learn is no less risky or contaminated than other forms of knowledge-making.

LEARNING TO LEARN: TOWARD AN ETHICS OF LISTENING/(RE)TELLING

What does it mean "to learn to learn" from others' stories in an ethical way, in a way that is mindful of the risk of harm that can be caused by academic discourse and actively works to mitigate it? I draw, in part, from community listening practices and researchers' own self-reflexive narratives in rhetoric and composition studies to begin exploring what this question makes possible. In "Decolonizing Community Writing with Community Listening:

Story, Transrhetorical Resistance, and Indigenous Cultural Literacy Activism," Rachel Jackson describes the Kiowa listening/storytelling practices that she engages in with her coauthor, Dorothy Whitehorse DeLaune, as "community listening," an effort not to allow the logic of argument to subordinate the collaborative meaning-making of listening to/telling stories. Jackson and DeLaune argue against a model of academic writing and scholarship that centers and structures a rational order that "settles" meaning. Instead, they argue for a "praxis of community listening" that "urges us to attend to the potential meanings and possible actions the story opens: the relationships between the past and the present situation, between peoples and places, between 'then and now' and 'us and them'" (40). This kind of listening involves a "shared responsibility" among listener/speakers for meaning-making that decenters an omniscient, disembodied academic voice from controlling the narrative.

In "Writing about Others Writing," Kate Vieira considers the harm caused by researchers who purport to listen collaboratively to the meaning of others' stories about writing but fall short. She writes, "Yet as much as I incorporated participants' words and perspectives and edits into my text, wasn't I, as an ethnographer, also inflicting something on someone with my writing?" (54). She learns through doing ethnographic research that ethical relationships in methodological analysis are formed in part by the researcher's owning their own methodological story, which for Vieira involved "dissecting participant stories . . . into axial codes" and then "stitch[ing] what had become pieces of data into a narrative whole" (56). Vieira's introspective and critical commentary on her own methodological processes of rational, ordered meaning-making in ethnographic research serves as a cautionary tale of one researcher's "dawning awareness of the potential for ethnographic harm" (58), and of the fact that research, no matter how collaborative, always causes some degree of harm, is always rooted in dynamics of power (55). Vieira attempts to counter this harm with a narrative self-reflexivity that works to name and mitigate uneven power between the researcher and the subjects of research.

Informed by and extending out from Jackson and DeLaune's community listening as a "shared responsibility" in collaborative meaning-making (42) and Vieira's call for researchers of writing to consider our role in "writing's legacy of abuse" (58), I engage in a praxis of listening/(re)telling in this book that was nurtured by my encounters with women learning English for resettlement and the representational ethics we navigated in speaking with and to one another. In that context, our storytelling and listening involved the following negotiations:

1. engaging with stories of experience, not as "data points" but as creative responses to tensions and contradictions of experience when experience is conditioned by the local along with the global;
2. understanding stories in a way that foregrounds their interventions in hegemonic discourse and recognizes them as challenges to our own historical imaginations;
3. attending to relations between the stories and the listeners' own experience and imagined histories in order to perceive, however partially, what is impossible to know, that is, others' experience, and to rethink the stories we tell of our own worlds in relation to others' stories, carefully; and
4. learning to learn from stories of experience as an ongoing, dialogic process beyond an initial encounter, a process that is different from data collection or knowledge extraction by a research authority or principal investigator, that is a *yielding to* others' stories.

Tracing these narrative negotiations through the transnational pathways of pre- and post-resettlement sites of adult learning, I have divided this book into two parts, each of which explores the listener/teller dynamics above in different ways: Part I centers others' stories with my story "standing nearby,"[4:] and Part II provides a multilayered contextualization of the stories from Part I that moves back and forth across resettlement locations and time.

To be more specific, Part I, Speaking with/to: "Living-English Stories," is composed of six chapters consisting of dialogues and stories among five women learning English for resettlement and me. The dialogues and stories are based on recorded interviews that took place across three Bhutanese refugee camps in Nepal from 2012 to 2013. Each chapter opens with a brief excerpt of dialogue that points to the theme of the chapter, followed by a biographical sketch of the speaker that provides context for the theme. The remainder of each chapter is composed of women's stories in translation. Their stories center on their language, literacy, and learning experiences before and during their protracted displacement as well as their hopes and fears around acquiring English for resettlement. Part I is an exercise in speaking with, listening to, and (re)telling women's stories of learning. It offers, performatively, through its mixing of genres and modes of writing (dialogue, biography, personal narrative, etc.), an argument about the possibilities and constraints of re-presenting stories in ethnographic literacy research, especially when storytellers and listeners do not share the same background or language. Part I explores the following questions: In what ways do storied re-presentations of learning evoke, enact, and affect knowledge that is situated and nonuniversalist? In what ways are these re-presentations always going to be partial, limited, and perspectival? What can be learned from partial stories?

While Part I demonstrates dialogic encounters with others' stories set in particular moments and locations within the pre-resettlement context of a protracted displacement, Part II, Learning to Learn: Situating Stories across Languages, Locations, and Time, offers a series of ethnographic snapshots and time lapses that move across pre- and post-resettlement locations in Nepal and the United States and work to further contextualize the stories of Part I. The snapshots depict scenes of language and literacy taking place on either side of the resettlement process, while the time lapses serve as critical, reflexive discussions of what it is I am learning to learn from others, collaboratively, through listening/telling as a layered and transformative research praxis. Learning to learn, I am listening back and reflecting, interstitially, between the snapshots

I took nearly a decade ago and the time that has elapsed. I am listening back and reflecting on the reverberations of encounters across locations of language and literacy learning in the United States and Nepal. And through these reverberations, I am learning to learn how to reframe transnational literacies as stories of absence (Chapter 7), sensuous coalition (Chapter 8), and lessons in living English (Chapter 9).

Together, the book's three parts reinforce an ethical vision for other ethnographers of literacy, as listeners and storytellers, who are rooted in ongoing processes of dialogic encounter, critical reflection, and reflexivity. In (re)presenting stories this way, my aim is to participate in a listening/(re)telling research praxis as a critical performance of possibility for new stories to emerge, a "rhetoric of possibility" in the context of transnational migration and protracted displacement (Calafell). Through storied re-presentations of experience, women construct a relationship to literacy that is deeply kinetic yet is a movement beyond the accumulation of literacy that frames notions of literacy success in the United States. Rather than evoke linear theories of literacy accumulation and development, the stories here evoke the uneven absences of literacy in women's lives and the critical positionalities that allow speakers and listeners to more freely explore what is possible outside of a progress narrative, the realms of possibility that language and literacy learning offer without being subject to it. Indeed, what this book claims is that the women who agreed to share their stories with me use the resettlement imperatives to learn English and become "literate" to do another kind of work, a kind of living-English work that brings to the surface stories of absence and deeper connections across past, present, and future, negotiating social change, impending resettlements, and deep divides between what language learning and literacy promise and what women know to be their experience of English and of literacy education. Situating their negotiations within the threshold space of an interminable waiting, waiting to be reconnected with loved ones, waiting to be resettled, waiting for the end of their protracted displacement, women *evoke, enact,* and *affect* their own moving literacies.

My hope is that the structural logic of the book will allow others to travel across different ways of knowing, listening, and (re) telling. My goal is to offer these encounters as layered accounts of global English language and literacy learning. In doing so, I take inspiration from an extensive body of poststructuralist and postmodern feminist, woman-of-color ethnography, "theory in the flesh" (Moraga and Anzaldúa), and rhetorical research methodology that understands narrative encounters not as a measure of the purity of empirical truth, but more like what Ruth Behar and Anna Tsing, both contemporary ethnographers of local-global relations, describe, respectively, as the "tangled roots" and routes of "contamination as collaboration" (*Translated Woman* 273; *Mushroom* 27–28). Stories, here, are what rhetorician Jacqueline Jones Royster calls "vital layers in a transformative process" (35). There is no lack of contamination in this kind of research, no clear agonistic demarcations, no holding abstract analyses above relational ethics or storied experience, no singular snapshot of a moment and a place. Instead, this book provides for "multiple streams of evidence" and "multiple loci for enunciating knowledge" in the form of dialogues, stories, snapshots, and critical time lapses that re-present, as they continue to reach for, an (im)possible ethics of learning to learn with and from others (Cushman et al. 14).

The living-English stories to which we are about to turn offer educators, researchers, and students of rhetoric, composition, and the teaching of English another possible research praxis for investigating the meanings of literacy learning in contexts of global migration. Speaking with/to these stories goes beyond the extractive work of self-abnegating empirical methods by rooting narrative encounters with others in situated dialogue, embodied collaborations, and learning to learn across vast chasms of difference.

PART I
SPEAKING WITH/TO: LIVING-ENGLISH STORIES

Part I

Speaking with/to: Living-English Stories

LIVING-ENGLISH STORIES DO MORE THAN DISTILL essences. They are expressions neither of speakers' internal worlds and singular identities nor of experience as a form of spontaneous cognition. Living-English stories, as Min-Zhan Lu and Iswari Pandey conjecture, do "word work" that is collaborative, creative, and critical. Living-English stories are responsive to the tensions and contradictions of language use in the context of a protracted displacement and other border crossings. Even more than telling or relaying linguistic information and resources grounded in experience, women's living-English stories evoke, enact, and affect a knowledge of moving literacies that has not succumbed to, nor resides outside of, but works in dialogue with the structural and emotional forces of prolonged statelessness. Women's living-English stories *evoke* lived experiences that are in tension with their expressed desire to learn. Their stories *enact* theory in the flesh that is both immediate and visceral, and, at the same time, exceeds experience as spontaneous, sensing, feeling consciousness. Women's stories open realms of experience through rhetorics of possibility: their stories are both an effect of, even as they *affect*, a kind of knowledge production that motivates and informs interventions in representational practices. More than providing a counterstance, stories of experience involve a rethinking and reframing of epistemological frameworks; experience becomes a resource for confronting, renarrating, and problematizing formative categories, possibilities, and constraints.

Thus, women's living-English stories, as stories of experience, participate in a kind of critical language work that points to deeper histories of absence, contradictions in their experiences of language and literacy learning, and questions about the value of English that bind their individual experiences of language and literacy learning together. Through the solidarity forged in the binds that tie women's experiences together, stories function as a form of living-English work that interrogates the assumptions about language, learning, and love implicit in my probing questions into women's educational backgrounds and investments in learning. Looking back on our encounters, now, from the position of a distanced observer who was once proximal, I can begin to perceive what I missed then, that the women who generously gave their time to speak with me were also extending an invitation through that dialogue to rework literacy hope and the violence of literacy. In this way, I am continuing to "learn to learn" by "speaking with and to" women through the listening to and retelling of these stories. I am learning to learn how women's stories *evoke*, *enact*, and *affect* a moving literacy in relation to resettlement imperatives, English-only ideology, and the myth of progress. I am learning to learn how I, as a storyteller-researcher, might engage with this "rush of stories" while acknowledging that I speak and write from a space of white privilege, that the locus of enunciation of my knowledge-making practices is the university, the English language classroom, writing and rhetoric studies, my own white body, my sexed and gendered, mobile and aging body as listener/storyteller speaking with/to women in diaspora. And, for Susmita, Suk Maya, Kali Maya, Abi Maya, and Kausila, learning English and telling stories with/to me is also an invitation to all of us to imagine *an-other* world of learning.[1]

Each of the chapters that follow attempts to make visible the "living-English work" of its speaker through dialogic performance. Stories are contextualized in vignetted conversations and biographical sketches and re-presented as part of an ongoing dialogue between storytellers and listeners. In addition, I include my own story here, contextualized in vignette and biography, standing nearby, and speaking with/to women and their stories. The italicized sections at the beginnings of the stories offer dialogic vignettes that point to the stories as part of an ongoing dialogue and collaboration, not only between me and storytellers, but also with the Spoken English Center guard amusedly eavesdropping while making tea the next room over or a local English teacher/translator intently listening, helping to broker differences in language and culture. The stories are part of a dynamic context that exceeds the limits of my focused inquiry. In writing up these narrative encounters, my goal was not only to take readers into women's experiences of learning English for resettlement but also to convey each of their perspectives as emerging from a unique set of circumstances, individual life stories, coalescing around each women's singular desire to join the Spoken English Center.

The short biographies help to contextualize women's experiences of literacy and schooling in the particularities of their lives as well as to illustrate the way women's stories emerge out of dialogue, so are always already part of a performance that is contingent, relational, and responsive to inequivalences among interlocutors. Women's stories are composed of narration from across various interviews, edited enough to maintain the confidentiality of participants, without losing cohesion or becoming wholly fiction. I represent women's perspectives in translation, but I do little to impose on these perspectives, analytically speaking. In other words, I do not attempt to superimpose on or extract a theory of literacy in motion from women's words and experiences, cutting up and parsing out bits of story and embedding these bits within academic discourse. Rather, I've decided to approach them with analytic restraint as a witness standing nearby, yet entirely complicit in the project of English language teaching, aware of its history and thoroughly enmeshed in what ethnographer Anna Tsing calls "contamination as collaboration"—meaning, that is, that there are no pure collaborations, only a "rush of stories as *method*" (27–28; 37).

Organizing Part I in this way, I want to suggest we listen to women's stories of learning and literacy experience as the basis for their contesting of literate subjectivities, for the ways in which their literacy learning operates as a performative intervention in the resettlement process and its imperative that they learn English. I want to suggest also that we hear how their stories evoke, enact, and affect a relationship to literacy that is kinetic, rather than mimetic, a movement within and beyond boundaries that calls into question the bounded subject of a literacy myth. Exploring both literate and nonliterate identities and subject positions within their stories allows women to frame their experience in unexpected ways and more freely play within the realms of possibility that literacy learning offers without being subject to it. Through the play of narrativizing their life and literacy experience, women seize hold of those dimensions of reading, writing, and language learning for which they consider themselves to have the most use— signing important papers, learning how to ask for directions— while challenging expectations that they become fluent in English. It is within this performance of possibilities and constraints that women emerge as agents and rhetors who, through their stories of experience and everyday performances, co-produce knowledge about the meaning of literacy.

1. *SIKNĒ ICCHĀ* / "THE DESIRE TO LEARN": SUSMITA

"If it's possible I would love to go to the US very soon because I don't like to stay here. But what to do?! The UNHCR won't take me at the said time!"

"Why learn English then?" I ask in Nepali.

"Now what did she say," Susmita mutters under her breath to the language center guard who sits nearby to watch the interview.

"Why are you learning English?" he says.

"Eh English!" she exclaims.

"We'll not stay in Nepal forever. That's why we must learn to use the English language. The people who left here already, three or four years ago, they all speak the things in English now, and the youth have gone from here. They don't speak Nepali anymore. They speak English. And, for the small ones, English comes very fast, but we old people have thick minds and English doesn't come to us.

"The small ones that have gone there are getting big now," she continues. *"They've forgotten Nepali talk, only English. If we go there, Nepali will not work. Yet, if we learn some English all that is accomplished is a kind of baby talk! If only I could write my name, it*

would be very, very good, at least that is what the people from there say. That is why I have the desire to learn."

Susmita, aged fifty-two, had never been to school before attending English class at the Spoken English Center in her sector of the Beldangi I refugee camp. As a young child growing up in Bhutan in the 1960s, she was "not admitted" to school by her parents. Besides this nonadmittance to the schools, there was no system of early education in her village and no forms of convenient transportation. The nearest school was too far to reach by walking. Instead of learning the "A, B, Cs," Susmita spent early life at her natal home working the fields as a *khētalo*, a field hand. Then, some time later, she became a farmer on her father-in-law's land. She describes herself as "illiterate," not able to read or write in any language. There was once an opportunity to learn, when Oxfam had a women's Nepali literacy program in the camp. But Susmita was managing three young children at the time and could not attend. The classes were short-lived, around eighteen months in duration. When Oxfam pulled out of the camps in the late 1990s, the Nepali literacy program ended as well. No other sustainable option for adult education and literacy would present itself again until resettlement, when Caritas Nepal in collaboration with local teachers began opening Spoken English Centers for adult learners. The centers cropped up throughout the camps during resettlement, taking over abandoned primary and secondary school structures that had closed as the camps began downsizing and merging together with the rapid emigration of camp residents being relocated.

Susmita had only been attending the Spoken English Center classes for a short time before we met. She says the reason she decided to begin taking classes was because of one "clever" friend who studied at the center before going abroad for resettlement and liked the experience of going to class. Like those of others in the class, Susmita's goals for learning focus on name writing and learning the English alphabet. Susmita would like to be able to write the names of her children as well. She is proud of the fact that she did not know how to write her own name before coming to the centers but is now able to provide her signature on important resettlement documents and on the camp lists when she goes to pick up her family's rationed allotment of rice from the Lutheran Services tent on the other side of the camp. It is an accomplishment that she mentions several times during my interviews with her.

Susmita believes education is important, especially for resettlement. She has heard from friends that life can be challenging on the other side of the process. Based on these conversations, she believes that most of the Bhutanese refugees in the United States get by with "sign language" and that as long as she knows enough English to put rice in her mouth, "*mukh bhaat*," everything will be okay.[1] In the dialogue excerpts below, Susmita discusses growing up in Bhutan with parents who did not see the necessity in educating their daughters. As Susmita narrates, she makes claims about why her parents decided not to educate her or her sisters, tying their decision to the perpetuation of patriarchal norms. Intertwined throughout her stories and dialogue with me are references to resettlement and the tensions Susmita faces in managing a family dynamic torn apart by the resettlement process.

Susmita's Reflections on Learning
Growing up in Bhutan

What can I say about Bhutan? In Bhutan, we were a family of five. After we came here, one of my daughters got married and my husband married another wife, and he's not here now. There is only one son, who brought a daughter-in-law. There is also a young daughter, who is not married, and she is reached the USA now.

In Bhutan, what did we used to do? The school was very far. There was no system to send anyone to school. There was only to look after the cows and work in the field. That we used to do.

There was no school. Only a few people's children used to go to school. School was very far. We were not near to the school. In someone's family, having many people, they might send children to school, but we had very few family members. Because of the work at the house, we didn't get chance to go to school, and also it was said that girls are not allowed to go to school. They used to say that girls should not be taught but only the boys, and my brothers were the only ones taught.

There were two brothers and three sisters. My sisters are in Bhutan itself, and I am the only one to stay here. All others are there, and I am the only one stuck here.

In the village, the army used to come, and fearing that, we left.[2] Many people were arrested from the village. It was difficult to sleep at night. We feared about if we would be caught by the army. Because of that we fled to the jungle, slept there. Sometimes it used to rain. Because of the fear, I didn't sleep. I didn't eat nicely.

How much tension there was!

We had to go to the jungle for shelter. We used to get wet because of the rain. How could we stay there? All the people from nearby villages started going, and we planned. Anything may happen, we should go. All the friends were going, we would not be able to stay there. They used to come at night. If we were trying to eat, they used to come at night in a group and we used to fear a lot! It was so dangerous in our village, too.

So, we came to Nepal, and we spent many years. But Bhutan was so good for us. My sisters and my parents' families are still there in Bhutan. Sometime before, I went there to meet them.[3] Sometime before, my sister came here to visit me. If we go there, my family will be terrified. My family said, "The villagers will see you, and you will be arrested!" How can we go back to Bhutan? Though we love the birthplace and all the fun we had there, everyone from the village is coming here.

Very few people go back. It's not good to stay there now. It's very sparsely located now, one house is here, other is *very* far! Also, if people have planted anything in their fields, it's eaten by wild pigs! I don't like to stay there! Most people have left. The village is full of plants, and it is jungle now. It's a very thick forest now, because many people left that place and only a few are there. It's not good to live there. Though the system is good there for electricity, drinking water. Even from the rocky mountains, electricity is provided to people. There is no power cut in Bhutan.[4] For the whole night *jadadadada*, the sound of electricity can be heard!

We faced difficulties in our times. We have to go to fetch water, walking a long distance, and we used to burn the light to get there. Now it's very easy. Now they are planting cardamoms and oranges, and they sell that and they use that money to eat. But what to do with those good things?! The law is very strict. It is not possible to stay in the same place and work, but they are forced to go to work wherever the *Drukpas* allocate them.[5] They have to reach where they are asked to go. And also, people who go from Nepal and India are not allowed to stay there. If we go there, we'll be arrested. If we secretly stayed for one or two nights, it's okay. But they have to bear the punishment, though! They could be chased out from there! They could be taken out from the country! They won't be allowed here. Where should they go?

That is the situation. It is very difficult. We love them very much. They are afraid there. Why to stay there? It was like that. Bhutan is the birthplace and there is love for that. The feeling is very good, but we are afraid. Why to go there? We have love inside, but we are not allowed to enter. Our families fear that if the government sees us, they will be arrested. Last year when we were there, they hid us inside the house. They feared that the government might see us. They were frightened and kept us inside one room. We were not allowed to talk too much or walk outside, and they feared and kept us hidden. The place is like that.

On Learning English for Resettlement

Learning the English language is like that. I did not know before. They didn't let us to study. There was no condition to read also. Even after coming here to Nepal, I didn't get a chance to study because of the children and the things at home. There was Oxfam, but I didn't get chance to go there. Now I feel many different things, but I didn't get sense at that time. Finally, I have got the sense, now, at the time when I am going to die, to study!

Before when I was young, the sense did not come. If I had studied at that time, I would have read these things nicely! But just now, in January, it has been one year now. Actually, it has been running one and a half years, I am only knowing that baby talk for English. Only baby talk and not writing. I only know a few numbers and can only recognize a few letters. I only know a little bit, how to write my name and do a signature. It came only that much. I can say, it came. What can I do? Before, I didn't know if we would be taken abroad, and I did not study. Only I thought, this Nepali could work, and there was nothing that said we would be taken abroad at that time. I see it now, in this way, people are taken abroad. If only I had studied earlier! I didn't know if we would be taken abroad, only thought that we would stay in Nepal. "It will be given, and we will simply stay and eat here," I said. Now I am regretting. Now the people are being taken from here continuously. People are going in vehicles continuously. They are being taken in seven or eight vehicles at a time.

It is very important to know English language. I did not know at the time and my mind didn't work, but now, it is happening like this. I heard that I can do any type of work and eat! One who doesn't know English and was illiterate reached there, there will be no communication even though we can work and eat.

I hear that people are doing and eating even by the sign of hands. We will easily understand this means this and that means that [with hand gestures]. Maybe, I will know to see the number plate of vehicle, house number and to see signboard. Our relatives have gone there, they may teach to do this thing or that thing, they will also teach us, and we have to follow these things to do. It's difficult to go from here but we will know easily. Though may not know more things, but a little bit I may know. I will understand as per the place.

The one who went there already said to do this thing in this way. In English, if they say, "This means this," we will come to know those things a little bit. When they take us from here, we will not be lonely over there. There, they are our Nepali people. They may not give us a job directly, but they may send us to school instead.

Now what can I do? All the people are going day by day for resettlement. My son and daughter are gone, and my own relatives are gone. Why to stay here, seeing whose face? We will not be taken back to Bhutan. I hear that it is very good in the US to eat and drink. There is no smoke, no dust. The *saag* is very good and available there, not like here in Nepal. They say, "It's very nice here! We are eating very good things there!" They are getting stronger, and we here are eating this dust and dirt. We're seen like this [Susmita gestures toward herself, swinging her arms up and down the length of her body in a disparaging way].

I am urged to go, but it is not possible. By this time, we would have already reached there, but now it is like this. If I die here, I will not be able to meet my children! What to do?! My children, my relatives are all gone. They are not taking fast enough. It would be nice if they would take us faster. Why to live here? Rainwater enters inside the hut. The government has stopped giving us bamboo. There is no one to keep the house. I have difficulties. The pole that keeps the house standing is almost destroyed. The house will fall down soon. How can I fix the house? I have no money.

People go from here and there, and I am alone. It is not good staying here all alone. There will be theft and robbery. It is dangerous to sleep at night. People will come at night to kill. People are very few now and located farther apart. There is fear here now. I have the feeling to reach the US as soon as possible, but what can I do about it?

"Coming and Going"
About America, some say it's good there and some say it is just okay. We have to work there. You can't not work. The work is easier, but we must have to follow time strictly. You are not allowed to sleep in the morning as you wish. And also, we are not allowed to talk with the friends for a long time, only on the weekends. And, we must have to go for work regularly. And, the one who is not able to go for work, the one who is not able to work, those must have to go to learn language. Language is compulsory.

I am illiterate, maybe it is difficult for me to learn about the job and to understand the language there, but we must have to learn the things of there. Here I have studied a little bit. If only I could remember what I studied here! I don't have a good mind! If I stay without work, my age is not suitable there. Only after sixty-five years, people get benefits.[6] My age is not suitable. I heard that for six months, the government will look after us nicely. After that, we have to do work.

Coming and going, coming and going, we'll learn one or two things. We may know some words by speaking and will be able to communicate like you. You are doing like that by coming and going, and we'll understand your talking. Now you are speaking in Nepali talk. Just like you, we will know English. I am feeling like that reaching there. You are coming to Nepal and coming and going. You are knowing many things. You are knowing from other people's speaking, without studying the language, and when we go there, we will learn from other people's talking.

By listening to others' way of talking, we will learn. Even if we do not write with the hands. I have much hope, thinking like that. You are speaking Nepali talk, and we are understanding, but also not understanding a few words. In the same way, English will come to us.

2. MA APHNAĪ LĀGI SIKCHU / "I LEARN FOR MYSELF!": SUK MAYA

Suk Maya describes what learning to read and write in English has been like for her. She describes her experience in the context of resettlement and being able to study English in the centers before her resettlement date comes:

"If I get chance to study here until I have to leave for resettlement, I will be very happy. I have some regret because I still can't make sense of English. I know every letter, but I don't know words. I am waiting. When will the sense come? I am thinking it will come one day.

"Learning this way is for myself. If I am lost also, if I am able to see the signboards, from here this side, from here that side, it will okay. Still, I can't make sense of those words, ma'am! What to do? I know all the letters, but I can't read words. What all those letters mean, that I don't know."

Suk Maya was sixty years old at the time of our first meeting. In our talks, Suk Maya recounts a tricky resettlement process. There is some problem with her case, but the narrative of this is hard to follow. There are multiple grown children, some resettled, others who have integrated into local communities through "intermarriage," when someone from the camps marries into a local family. There is at least one adult daughter who is resettled with her husband's family in the United States. This daughter calls Suk Maya often and begs her to attend classes at the Spoken English Center. She pleads with her mother to "please learn English, and then come quickly to the US." But Suk Maya can't speed up her resettlement process. At the time I knew her, Suk Maya seemed to be living in a state of indefinite waiting. "Who knows what the future will bring?" she says.

I ask Suk Maya to tell me about her childhood in Bhutan and her early memories of schooling. She brings the conversation almost immediately to the subject of her early literacy denial. According to Suk Maya, despite being successful as independent farmers and cattle herders, her parents were not interested in schooling. She describes them as *"agyanta,"* ignorant, a product of their time and tradition. She is quite derisive of her parents' decision not to educate her. To her, this decision was pure ignorance.

"They used to say, '*Gāʼharūlāʼī jhundyāʼēra!* By hanging up the cows (I could go to school)!'" Suk Maya laughs. She repeats this story several times in my interviews with her.

She likens her teachers at the Spoken English Center to "true" parents, not like her biological parents, whom she describes as "duplicate," poor quality. She says this is because her teachers have nurtured her ability, while her biological parents, despite being incredibly wealthy compared to others, did not find the time to send her to school. Suk Maya views this nonadmittance to school as a social-structural and family issue; most girls in her village were not educated. There were a few, but her family was not one of those families that educated its daughters. Out of ten sisters, she recalls, none were admitted in the local school. There was one brother who went to school. Using the English loan word, "clever," Suk Maya describes this brother as cunning. He used his education to get ahead. Suk Maya links his recent resettlement to his being educated. Ruefully she adds, only the "deaf and dumb" have been left behind.

But she remains cautiously hopeful that eventually she will be able to read a little bit of English, enough to get by in the world outside of the camps. She tells me, "English is for everything," especially for reading signs and not getting lost after resettlement. These ideas about English are repeated throughout our conversations and were reinforced in her English class by her teachers through dialogue exercises on how to ask for directions and word lists connected to food, shopping, and kitchen items among other "survival literacies." Indeed, the connection between English and survival was pervasive. Not only Suk Maya but many of her peers claimed that "English is for everything," for every basic need. By comparison, it was common to hear that Nepali was nothing special, only to be used for "saying things inside the house."

"If only I had known it is very good to learn English at twenty years old or forty! But now I am sixty and I am learning. Maybe I don't know much, but my wish is to continue learning until I die. I can't imagine what the future holds! But I know all the [English] letters. Others have said to me that I will know one day."

Matter-of-factly she says, gesturing back toward the Spoken English Center quad and adjacent classrooms, "I came up from there, from grade A."[1]

Suk Maya on Life, Work, Schooling, and Resettlement
In Bhutan, we have all the work to do. We have to look after the baby—sometimes we have to keep it on the floor or in the cradle.

We have to look after the cows, the buffalo, also the goats and sheep. And we have to do our own work and friends' work, "*kethala*," in the fields. But here there is nothing. There, in Bhutan, we must have to do up to seven types of work, but there is no work here, just to cook and eat, and bring the water, and to make small pieces of firewood that we burn in the stove. We have no other work. We used to do seven types of different work in Bhutan before we sleep, but if I expect the same thing here of my daughter-in-law, she will probably tell me, this old woman is going crazy! We will be considered crazy if we say like that! Eh! We used to do seven different kinds of work before we go to sleep, but here we just cook and eat and come to language class.

Being a daughter-in-law in Bhutan there were many responsibilities, ma'am. Waking up early in the morning, we have to clean *lotta* for a long time until they shine.[2] We used to carry water, and fetch all the *lotta*, and prepare tea, and give it to father- and mother-in-law. We used to carry and keep pitchers of water for father- and mother-in-law to wash their faces. Only after that, I used to prepare food for the children and look after them. Sometimes my mother-in-law would help, but most of the time I, myself, had to do that work. School was far. If father and mother had known at that time that life would be like this, then they would have sent us to school, and it would be easy to read now. But they were rich by money, not by education. There was not the sense to invest in education. If there was money, that was enough for them. My parents gave to each of their daughters one *tola* of gold and a pregnant cow.[3] To all ten of us, they cut pig and sheep, and made a big wedding. For Brahmins, they gave sheep to eat! If one of my sister's cows died, they gave another one! It was our dowry. One *tola* of gold and a pregnant cow. Two were given, double, as the cows died! Though they were good parents, they didn't allow us to study. I had two good brothers, but the clever one of the two is gone now for resettlement. Only the deaf and dumb are left behind.

Now, it is like this, ma'am: My son-in-law has gone to Saudi Arabia and has left my daughter simply staying there in the village alone. If he comes back, who knows what will happen at that time. People from the IOM came and asked me about my son-in-law, and I said that he had gone abroad. They wrote that down and took it with them.[4] Who knows what will happen to my process because of that. Without my son-in-law, maybe there will be no process. The people at the IOM said that. It is four years that is he staying in Saudi Arabia and our process is incomplete. He says, if we are going to leave, why not come to Saudi Arabia, but all my sons are here! Other people's sons are sensible and have left their families to go for resettlement, but we come from a place that isn't like that. My sons are not like the ones who think, let's leave our parents and go! Many people are crying nowadays because it's happened to them. Someone's son went to one country. Someone else's went to another country. But not my sons because they are fully concerned about their sister! We have no feelings to split from each other. It's good to go together to the same place, isn't it? My sons are simply staying here and there. There is one nearby in Siliguri and sometimes he says, maybe you could come here, Mother.[5]

If I get a chance to learn how to read before I leave for resettlement, then I will be very happy. I have some regret because I haven't learned until now. Now, I know all the letters of the [English] alphabet, but I don't know how to read words. I have dedicated myself to learning. I give my time, my effort, my prayers, but I just don't have that much memory for English. I am waiting for the sense to come, but I wonder if I *can* learn. I keep telling myself, it will come one day. Learning this way is for myself. I am learning so that I do not become lost. I am learning to be able to read the signboards, from here on this side, from there on that side. If I can do that, I know I will be okay. But, learning how to read these things doesn't come easily, ma'am! What can I do? I see these letters, and I know them, but how to make sense of them, what they mean, I don't know.

3. *(MALAAĪ) ALI-ALI (ANGRĒJĪ) ĀUCHHA / "JUST A LITTLE (ENGLISH) COMES (TO ME)"*: KALI MAYA

"I came to the Spoken English Center and little by little I have learned: ABCD, conversations. They came to me. I want to know more, learn more, because study is never over. Sometimes if I ask my husband for help, he helps me, but sometimes he scolds me, 'You are going to school for a long time and still you don't know anything. This means this, and that means that,' he says, 'and you still don't know these things even after studying for a long time!'"

"Eh," shrugs Kali Maya, "I forget quickly."

"I am trying. I am learning. I wonder whether someone will say to me, you studied for a long time and you can't come to school anymore. At that time, I will have nothing to say. But if they say, you are allowed to come to school, and it is your desire, I will continue to learn. If I get a chance, I will continue to learn until I go there.[1] That is my desire."

Kali Maya, forty-eight, describes herself as self-sufficient, better than her husband at some types of work. She says the daughter who resettled in the US is also like this: strong. Unfortunately, Kali Maya is stuck "date waiting," uncertain of when or even if she will be reunited with her daughter through the resettlement process. The family's case file has been put on pause because of an unfortunate incident involving Kali Maya's son, who was jailed for starting a fire in the camp. While she waits for the reprocessing of her case file to begin, Kali Maya spends most of her time caring for two extended family members who are deaf, and, in her spare time, attending English class. Kali Maya studied in Oxfam for four months during the late 1990s and learned to write a letter in Nepali at that time. She remembers writing a letter to her husband while he was living out of the camp. But over the years, she stopped writing and gradually forgot how. She stopped attending Oxfam because she had young children at home at that time, but there was also a feeling of purposelessness. She wondered at the time, "What is the purpose of my study? What can *I* do?" Kali Maya has attended English classes in her camp sector's Spoken English Center for nearly one year. After her first four-month course, she moved up from Grade A, considered to be a preliterate class, to grade B for beginners, and because of her rapid progress is known as a fast learner.

For Kali Maya, learning to read and write now is a matter of integrity, independence, or "to be able to stand on our own legs," as she puts it.

Kali Maya's Thoughts on Being Born in Bhutan, the "Process," and Learning English between "Here" and "There"

On Being Born in Bhutan
I was born in Bhutan. I grew up there and got married. I brought my elder son from there itself. My husband was a mechanic, before, but he doesn't have any certificate from Bhutan. My parents were farmers and me, too. I did not go to school when I was young. At first, we were in Gelephu and later we were shifted to Danabari. Anyway, it is within the same district but different block.[2] Maybe for some reason I was not admitted to the school. I was not admitted, but I used to look after goats and take buffalo for grazing. I collected firewood and in the agricultural season I went to the field for rice planting. I also collected grass.

I didn't go to school. Maybe what happened was that my parents did not admit me. The school was not so far. It was near. Maybe at the time it was like that. There was also a fee. That is why my second brother was the only one admitted. My elder brother did not study. He was a conductor and finally he became a driver, and, while going out, he spoke to people and knew things. And then the youngest sister came here to Nepal and studied. She studied outside on the grounds and in the jungles under the sisoo trees because there was no school built at that time.[3]

My youngest sister studied up to class 6 and she got married. Now she is the mother of two children. I am the second daughter.

I have an older sister. Among three brothers, my oldest brother left the house, and I used to wonder if he would come back to meet me. He came once. He came with his wife, two sons, and a child in the womb. He was such an angry man. He was staying outside, and his census was canceled because he had left for many years. My brother was tall, and he said that he was living in Kashmir. He returned one more time and after that he hasn't come back. My other two brothers, father and mother, and sisters, they all went to the US.

Actually, my husband used to stay with his uncles because my husband's mother died when he was young, and my husband's father remarried. My husband's father was lost, and he started to stay with his uncle. We were poor and there was an old grandmother. Whatever she said, others had to follow. We were staying with the uncle's family, and they gave us a kitchen. When my husband went to work as a driver, I stayed at home and looked after our small child. I used to buy rice with my husband's income. We used to eat like that.

We were very sad to leave Bhutan. Whatever the reason was for our leaving, it was our motherland. I was sad. At that time, I wondered what would happen? Where would we go? I cried and shouted. But we came here to Nepal. We got asylum here. Only three of us left Bhutan, though my husband was a number 1 in the census.[4] We thought that everyone would go, so we came out of the country just the three of us with the child. My parents left the country after some time.

The "Process"

Actually, about my process, medical is already done.[5] My son suffers from jaundice. At one point, his life was out of order, and he left school at grade 7. Now he is addicted to some bad things like drugs. Our process was stopped, but we didn't know about it. Before the medical exam, they asked what drugs he was taking and at that time we said he smoked cigarettes only because we didn't know that he was taking drugs. But later, during the medical appointment, he was found using drugs and that is why our process stopped. A month later, we put him in rehab. We were told our process would move fast again once my son gets out of rehab, but then after some time, our file was placed in suspension for up to one year for cheating at the time of our interview.[6] When my son finally did get out of rehab, he got married, and the age of my daughter-in-law is not suitable for marriage.[7] Eventually, my son and daughter-in-law became separated, and she left with her brother to Massachusetts in the US with vulnerable status.[8] So, we are staying like this.

We are sometimes called for follow-ups in IOM. Sometimes we don't go because of illness. Maybe next week we will be called there because there will a doctor from Biratnagar who specially deals with my son. The doctor said maybe it will take quite a long time. Also, he gives some advice to my son about being a good person and not taking drugs. So, he said that your problem will be solved after one year, and after that your file will go to US, and if they recommend from there, then you will go. Anyway, my son must be good. Today is exactly one week that he received his first treatment from his doctor, and he is doing okay. Our son is in the house, and he is okay, but now our youngest daughter is trying to separate her case from our file and go on her own for resettlement.

Learning between "Here" and "There"

I am wondering how can I work there and live there and, also, how can I adjust with the environment and culture there? I think like that. That place is such a place that we haven't gone before. Now how can we do and live there? I feel like that. Also, if I could take my sons there, their life would be nice. They would be able to stand on their own feet. Maybe for my sons it is nice, but for us, I don't know.

Anyway, we'll have to do something to live, and it won't be like here, just eating whatever is provided by the organizations. Maybe I will get a type of job there, though I'm not educated. I have hope because unless I'm sixty or sixty-five, I'll not get benefits, so I must have to work.

I tell my friends, please come to school. If we learn something we will be able to teach our children. Also, I say to old grandmothers: please come learn English! Because they will have grandchildren who will help them to learn. And, some are coming, but some left the school because of some problems. There are many friends now. I used to message everyone before and in the beginning of the sessions.

Oxfam was a long time ago. I studied Nepali there for eighteen months. That was my first school. When I was in Bhutan, I used to go to school to cook for the nursery children. When I was with the children at that time, I learned A, B, C, and A for apple. Only that much. But after coming to Nepal, I struggled a lot for eighteen months to study. At that time, I also had a small child. The youngest son now. I used to carry my son and leave him with my father-in-law's brother and my mother-in-law's mother. I studied like that for eighteen months. I haven't forgotten what I read at that time, but I don't remember everything. I can read in Nepali. I can even read correspondences and I can write my name in English and Nepali and also the names of my family members. Also, English was taught there within eighteen months, and we learned half English and half Nepali. After learning there, we had to read our medical card by ourselves. It was like that, to be able to read the medical card.

I have attended classes at the Spoken English Center for two years, starting from grade A. I am in grade C now. It is interesting. I didn't get a chance to study when I was young. My parents didn't admit to school. In the meetings when there are some dignified people, like Father speaking in English, I couldn't understand anything.[9] That is why I joined the language center. My friends said, language class has started, why don't you come with us? And I felt shy. I don't know anything, I used to think, so how can I go there? But they said, all are like us, they don't know anything.

At first, I denied to go, saying that I didn't know anything. But a neighbor's sister told me that the lessons were taught nicely there, and she convinced me. After that, I registered myself for classes, and now I come regularly to the school and know many things.

Actually, I am learning this so that it will be easier to live there in US. I will not understand that place or be able to reply to people. Their tongue there is different. But that is why I am studying here, thinking that it will be easier for me there. I must learn there, too, of course. English is useful everywhere, even if we stay here, so it's important to study it and understand it. If someone is speaking, if we even have a simple understanding of what is being said, it's a great thing. That is why I learn, why I study.

4. GOTHALĀ BHŌKALĀ MĀRALĀ / "THE HUNGRY SHEPHERD DIED": ABI MAYA

I ask Abi Maya, "What are your goals for learning English?"

She replies, "English is for going abroad, but even if we stay in Nepal, we need to know English. While speaking Nepali, we use some English words, but we do not speak correctly! To speak correctly, we must have to come to the school of language. For example, if we do something and someone says to us, 'You are very stupid!' Like in Nepali, the word is 'raddi,' but in English, isn't it that you are dirty? You are poor, isn't it? It means, like, you are useless and dirty!

"It happens!" She says, "To say that. Not to understand.

"For the purposes of when it is said to us, for that reason we should learn English."

As we talk, I am left wondering if Abi Maya will continue her studies abroad, even after support from the government has expired and the time for becoming a citizen has come and gone, usually within the first five years. I ask, "After five years in the foreign country, will you go to language class?"

"I will go!" Abi Maya states emphatically. "Learning to read and write is very important for us because like the old proverb of the hungry shepherd died—go Thalā bhōkalā māralā—we are able to do. We are able to read and write a little bit. We can understand that much only."

Abi Maya was fifty-one at the time of our interview. Like many of the other women her age attending classes at the Spoken English Centers, she had not been formally educated. She was married young into a polygamous family structure in which she was the second wife. As subsistence farmers, her family struggled to cultivate the rocky and treacherous land along the border between Bhutan and India. Abi Maya recalls spending much time in the fields, clearing rocks and stones and tilling soil for the millet, rice, corn, and bitter grains that were just enough for her family to eat. Abi Maya's family met their survival needs that way until the agitation began. At that time, Abi Maya recalls feeling trapped between political parties and their agendas. She says, "There was quarreling and disputes and the eruption of parties. There were two parties inside and outside. If we joined the outside party, the inside party would arrest us, and if we stayed with the inside party, the outside party would arrest us."

Eventually, the family fled Bhutan, but Abi Maya wonders if leaving was the right decision. She tells me, "Being illiterate without any sense, even the smallest person could frighten us. Without education, there was nothing inside our sense. If we have known before, and could be sure they wouldn't kill us, we wouldn't have left the country. But we had to leave because of fear."

In a conversation with her peers late in the final spring of my studies in Nepal, Abi Maya relays the story of the hungry shepherd (*go Thalā bhōkalā*). A shepherd goes into the wood and runs out of rice. With no other recourse, the shepherd sends a transcribed message home with a well-intentioned passerby. The messaged was intended to show how the shepherd was starving and was in need of rice, but the message that was received relayed instead that the shepherd had died of starvation. The misunderstanding was a result of mistranslation. The shepherd's colloquial ways of talking left off important verbal conjugations marking differences between the shepherd having died of starvation and the shepherd about to die of starvation.

Abi Maya's Reflections on "the Agitation," Early Education, and Learning for Resettlement

From before we were very poor. My land was rocky, and we struggled a lot to make the field good from there. And then, eventually, we were able to do. We made a field of one *muri* rice seed ready to be planted. We cleared the rocks and stones. Digging that, and then there was millet, rice, and maize. Also, *fapar* was there.[1]

The land was steep. We were near the border of Bhutan and India and down from us was the riverside where we had our land. Yearly, the river cut through a small portion of our land.

Anyway, there was good cultivation of rice there. It was good and sufficient for us to eat. Whatever we cultivated was sufficient for our family. We were saying, we don't have to depend on any other family for survival, but then the agitation began.

There was quarreling and disputes and the eruption of parties. There were two parties, inside and outside. If we joined the outside party, the inside party would arrest us, and if we stayed with the inside party the outside party would arrest us. It happened like that, and we fear that and could not tolerate it.

Then we were told, "You are a number 7."[2] We didn't understand. "Who and what is this number 7?" we asked. They used to say, "something, something," as we didn't go to the office. Only our husbands used to go. We didn't understand.[3] We thought even coming to the house we will be arrested! Some even said, "You should go away from here! Otherwise, you will be killed."

When such things were happening, we fled from there. We were categorized as number 7 by the *Drukpas*. And they compelled us to fill out a form to leave. Also, they gave us some money for traveling. Many people fled, but *we* were taken out for being in the number 7 category.[4] From time to time, *they* used to come asking, "Your date for leaving is now, when will you leave?"[5]

Time and again, they came, and we were given the date to go, and on the same date we left.

After that we came and stayed in India, but because some of my relatives were in Nepal, we were taken here and placed as refugees.[6] I had two young children at that time, one son, one daughter. When we stayed there in India, they passed away.

I didn't get the chance. My parents gave me to another when we were young. It is also to another's husband. There was already a wife, *jethi mathi thyo*. So, my parents gave me a *jethi mathi*.[7]

We got many problems and gave birth to children and cared for them. Staying like that, the agitation began, and then we didn't have to flee, but we were told to go out in a good way.

We didn't take anything with us. Everything was left inside Bhutan: our millet, maize, rice. We didn't have much maize, but we sold all the rice and millet. And then, we left from there.

We didn't understand that people were going to Nepal at that time when we were staying in India. Staying in India, like that, after some time we were taken here.[8]

We were afraid at that time, being illiterate. Being illiterate without any sense, even the small person could frighten us. Without education, there was nothing inside our sense. If we had known that they wouldn't kill us, we wouldn't have left Bhutan, but we were afraid and very innocent. We were frightened by the treatment of others.

As farmers, we didn't understand what was happening. We only used to go to the market, not school. Only my older brother could read. I never even saw the school where my brother used to go! Some people in our village led their children to study, but not us. Even from a very young age, we were sent to work in the field to look after the animals, cows, goats. We worked outside. It was hard work. To speak honestly, we didn't get a chance to enjoy life or even take time to eat.

I went to Oxfam for eighteen or nineteen months and I learned Nepali. I can't write, but I can read a little. Though we were taught a little English, it went right out of mind!

After a long time, I am learning at the Spoken English Center. Now, I understand a little English. I can write my name. I know some words for kitchen items, the names of one or two fruits and vegetables. Only a little English.

It is said, "If we speak one thing, we already have forgotten another." If we had more time to study at home, without household responsibilities, the learning would come fast. But what we learn here, we forget it immediately. It happens due to the problems and tensions we face. Because of that, we can't speak much. We would like to read more, speak more, but for us, if we think one thing, our mind will be somewhere else. That is why our English is weak.

My daughter has already gone through resettlement. "Mother," she says, "study nicely. Learn English at the language centers and then come." My children are telling me that I should learn English, otherwise I will have difficulties in the US. That is why even though we may have problems at home, we must come to the language centers to study. I heard that if we are not able to learn English well and not able to speak it, we will not do well there. We won't be able to work. So, we must stay interested. We must study!

In Bhutan, English was also taught. Dzongkha, English, and Nepali was taught there. In India, Bengali, Hindi, English, and Nepali will be taught. There is everything in India except Dzongkha. Here in the camps, Dzongkha, English, and Nepali is taught. It is important to learn, though, actually, there is no reason to learn Dzongkha because we will never be able to go back to Bhutan. We have to go to America where they only speak English. There is no work done in Nepali there, either!

For these reasons, even old people should learn English. Old people must be able to hear and talk and understand the language. Even though we are old, we have to learn, too. If we don't learn, then our children will only speak to English people. Everyone in my family will be able to speak English. My children. My daughter-in-law. My grandchildren. All will speak English, but we old people will not understand. "What are they saying?" the old people will say, "I do not understand!"

We must keep in mind that our children will be learning and speaking English, and if we don't learn, we won't be able to understand them.

After reaching America, it will be my job to do whatever work there is to do, even to stay home with the grandchildren and look after them. Cooking food, eating, keeping house. We must do those things, too, right? We have to teach the very small children how to speak, how to do. Tell them not to quarrel or do bad things. We have to teach the small children how not to be dirty, not to speak badly but to speak good things. We have to teach them like that.

Now, for us, it is like this to write: our eyes will be poor, and our hand isn't fast. Writing does not come quickly or accurately. That is why, if we could learn to speak and hear the language, we could be quite free. I could go anywhere and, if you were to say something to me, I would understand you. If we learn to speak and hear English, we could have some sense.

Though we are old, we study to understand. We are not able to write that much or correctly. But anyway, we must study.

5. *GHARKŌ SUKHA-DUKHA JASTAI HŌ* / "(LEARNING ENGLISH) IS JUST LIKE THE JOYS AND SORROWS OF HOME": KAUSILA

"To tell or not to tell?" Kausila thinks about it and then says, "There are two children from outside . . . ."

Kausila's daughter has disappeared and left two children behind from a broken marriage to a local guy who is also nowhere to be found. Kausila hasn't heard from her daughter for over a year and half and suspects that she has found some work in Kathmandu. Kausila is afraid to report the children to the UN High Commissioner for Refugees (UNHCR), fearing that her process will be stopped, and she is afraid to give up the children to the father's parents, who live in a village nearby, fearing that the grandmother, who is the father's stepmother and not a blood relation, won't take good care of them.

"My daughter has children," says Kausila, "as though she were piling up garbage!"

Still, Kausila makes time for learning English, certain that as long as she doesn't report the children, her resettlement process will continue along without interruption. She is set to leave the children in the camp under the care of a young auntie, but she doesn't get into the details of that relationship. She is expecting to be resettled to Australia, where her other daughter lives now. Her resettlement date could come at any time.

"Sometimes I feel like, how would it be there? I close my eyes and I imagine a place that is very clean and shiny. But when I open my eyes, it's gone.

"Learning at this age is a house of happiness and suffering, a blessing and a curse," Kausila says. "I have an interest to study English. I like to read. But now, my eyes are weak. I have to use glasses to read. When I'm reading, I understand, but later, I forget. It is difficult and forgetting happens."

Kausila was fifty years old at the time of our interview. Kausila, like most women of middle age living in the camps, claims that she was never formally educated. Besides a brief time of taking the Nepali literacy classes provided by Oxfam, Kausila's access to educational resources has been uneven, interrupted. It was not until the time of our meeting, on the cusp of Kausila's resettlement, after nearly twenty years of living in displacement in the Bhutanese refugee camps in Nepal, that Kausila has finally got the chance to learn with some consistency, though learning does not come easily now. Our conversations mostly revolve around this point—"*Gharkō sukha-dukha jastai hō!* (Learning English) is just like the joys and sorrows of home!" says Kausila. "To be able to learn now, when I'm too old to remember anything!"

Kausila's life was, indeed, like a house of happiness and suffering, rife with paradoxes and contradictions of displacement. With every opportunity, there is a loss. The desire to learn later in life is muted by Kausila's experience of aging. Indeed, Kausila is acutely aware of the temporal relationship between cognition, her experience of biological aging, and mobility in the urgent contexts of a ramped-up resettlement process. The speeding up and slowing down, the warp and weft of time is palpable in her stories.

Kausila on the Desire to Learn

On Not Getting a Chance to Study

In Bhutan, we did not get a chance to study. The responsibility was farming, looking after cattle, and doing fieldwork. That was my responsibility. Because I didn't have an education, I couldn't go for a job. My responsibility was only that, to look after cattle, look after the children, cook, and clean the house. Fieldwork, cattle, that's all.

But since I was small, I was interested in learning to read. I made sure to admit my oldest son in the school as soon as he turned four. He was so small that he could barely walk on the road to the school, and he used to slip on the downward slope of the road. I used to carry him to school, though I also slipped on that road.[1]

The teachers in Bhutan used to say, only the one big enough to wrap one arm around the head and touch the opposite ear will be admitted to school.

A teacher argued with me, "Why are you bringing your small child to school? Other people who have children even bigger than your son do not bring them here!"

The teachers used to tell me, "The time is not suitable for your son to come to school because he isn't able to touch his ear!" But I said, "It isn't so! He will become habituated to school by staying with his friends and seeing the things at the school."

I convinced the teachers to admit my child, and they did. But my child did not walk himself to go there. I carried him up and down the road, sometimes slipping and falling along the way. If we slipped, we would fall to the bottom of the hill. Doing like that, I educated my child.

But now, my child is grown, and he is staying further from my house.

Now, it's okay. I have a daughter and a process for going abroad. I have an interest to study English. But I do not understand English as clearly as Nepali. I don't know why it is so!

In written Nepali there is a system of representation for vowels, *matra*, but in English there is no *mātrā*.[2] I heard that there is a book from which we will know English very fast. I have asked people from outside to bring that book to me, as I don't know where to get it here.

Learning to Read in Nepali, Then English

I am so interested to learn English! In Bhutan, I was not taught, but I was interested to study. After coming to Nepal, I heard that Oxfam was going to open. I was staying here in the camps, and a brother came and asked me, "Would you like to go to Oxfam?"

At first, he thought that maybe I had been educated before, and he went away without asking me if I wanted to join. I was interested to study at that time, and I wondered, is it possible to study at this age? I thought, I'll register myself and go to study.

I took the process a little further. I asked that brother what he was registering people for, and I asked him if he was looking for people to go to Oxfam. I asked him, "Why didn't you register me?" The man replied, "I thought you were educated. That's why I didn't ask you before." And then, I said to him, "Please register me. I want to read."

He registered me, and I was the first one to study from my sector. I was the only one from my sector to go, and I felt ashamed, and I would hide my books on the way to school.

Some educated people used to tell us, "Don't waste your time, children! Don't waste your time playing!" People used to tease me like that. So, I changed the way I walked to school, fearing that people would tease me.[3]

I studied Nepali nicely, and now I can read everything in Nepali. Whatever comes to me, maybe the *Mahabharat*, the *Devi Bhagat*, or any other big books. I can read those. I know how to read Nepali.

As I was interested in reading, I used to be at the top of my class. At that time, there was little English, and finally there were three English classes. But with some problems at home and with young children, and, also, with no husband, studying became a burden for me. Because of this tension and other things, I forgot most of what I studied in the English class.[4]

At first, we were taught a little bit of English, but they took great care to teach Nepali. English did not come that much, and they mostly taught Nepali. I studied there for eighteen months, totally. My husband came and went at this time, during the first seven months of my study at Oxfam. And then, he disappeared.

After that, I was alone, though my husband had been there when I first joined the school. He used to think that I was not going for study, but that I was going somewhere else. So, there were two different feelings about school between him and me.[5]

I studied Nepali in that way. I was interested to learn English, though, but I thought that I was too old to learn. It happened like that. But anyway, I am trying to learn now. For us, we are not too old to study.

Reflections on Learning English and Resettlement

The reason I study English is that when I go abroad, everything will be in English. It is like this. If we come to Nepal and know Nepali, it is very good. And, if we go abroad, we need English. Nepali won't work there.

That is why. That is why I am learning English. I was interested in learning English when I was young, but I didn't get the chance then.

Now, I am getting a chance to study, and later I will go to the foreign country where English is best and where it is needed. English is the main thing.

Sure, there are problems at home, but if I focus on such things, I won't find the time to come and learn. So, I make time and go to class. I feel it is important. Being able to know and speak English means, wherever I go, I can get along.

Knowing and speaking Nepali means only being able to get along in Nepal. For these reasons, I feel English is very useful, right?

I know many things in English now. I can tell me age, my name. I know how to say, I live here in Nepal. I like to learn about going to the vegetable market and meeting up with friends to socialize.

I want to speak English, as I do Nepali, fluently. But how? I don't know. It's a struggle for me to learn. I still don't understand when there are many people together, and they are all talking at once. I can't understand them. I would like to know and understand them. I feel like that.

My resettled children are telling me to study, but I don't get much encouragement from anyone else.

My resettled daughter says, "If you come to Australia, you must continue to study here. If you learn English while in Nepal, it will be good, and easy for you to live here. Living here, you will learn even more things. Even as an English teacher in Nepal, I am still learning!"

My daughter is studying English there, and I asked her if she could understand the teaching there, and she said, "We can understand everything very nicely!"

Sometimes I feel uncertain about the future. I wonder, how will it be? How is it? Who will be there? Maybe, it's good there for traveling. Maybe . . . . How is the place there? And maybe, it's a different world. I feel it may be a different world and very different from here. Probably, it is like what I imagine.

Maybe the houses are really nice, and I will be completely contented. Or maybe, it is awful, and I will faint and fall down with terror. I feel like that sometimes, too. But most of the time, I feel that it will be good to live there.[6]

I tried not going there, but finally I wondered, what would I do here? Sometimes I think that, where should I go from here? I think to myself, having had to leave Bhutan, why do we have to leave Nepal, too? Maybe, it would be better if I died. But what to do? My daughter is gone. She says it's nice and good in Australia. It is good. And if she says it is good, it will be good for me as well.

I miss her. Anyway, I love my children. She is gone, alone. There is no other reason for me to go except to be with her. No one else has gone to Australia from my parents' side. All others have gone to America. Others on my parents' side are gone there. My daughter has gone to Australia, and she is the only one from my own house to go there. We are here, but our process is also going on. Let's see when we will go. Maybe, we will go soon, maybe not. How will it be? Maybe, it will be okay.

To go to the place of my daughter makes me feel happy, but I wonder about the place, which I have never seen. I'm a little worried. Sometimes I think, how is it going to be there? Will there be problems? It's normal to feel that way.

Anyway, I'm happy now, and after going to Australia, I think that I will continue to study.[7]

6. STORYTELLER LEARNING AND DOING[1] / "LISTENING BACK": KATIE

I hadn't set out to find these stories. But they came. One right after the other. Rather than point me to evidence of women's desire to acquire and accumulate literate resources for their resettlement in English-speaking countries, they invite me into another kind of movement, into an engagement in the co-production of literacy hope and living-English work. Through the listening to/retelling of stories, I am speaking with and speaking to, and through this interchange, I am learning to learn that their investment in English for resettlement doesn't form as clear a trajectory as it might at first seem. And this was because learning English later in life in the midst of an actively unfolding, decades-long displacement was less about acquiring literate resources for enhancing the experience of global mobility than it was about learning to navigate the possibilities and constraints of connecting to and knowing others in the context of forced migration and its reverberations in resettlement.

I was thirty-three at the time these interviews were conducted, and it was my first time conducting ethnographic fieldwork in a systematic way abroad. At first, my conversations with women were stilted and awkward. Nepali felt like cotton balls in my mouth. The women who volunteered to speak with me would look at me quizzically before turning to their English teacher, a local female educator from the camps, who always sat close by, listening, witnessing, translating, participating, ready to step in when my language skills failed me. It was not for lack of trying to learn Nepali. I had been deeply immersed in the language since before my arrival in Nepal. I had spent months with former students back in Tucson reciting *Ka, Kha, Ga, Gha*, the Nepali alphabet, and learning helpful Nepali phrases and vocabulary. I memorized dialogues to make small talk and introduce myself. I learned all the names of my students' yet-unsettled family members who were waiting in Nepal to receive me as a guest and to help me with my research in exchange for English lessons.

When I arrived in Nepal, I stayed at the home of my Nepali teacher's brother, who was living outside of the camps with his wife and children while petitioning for resettlement. The brother had two young daughters in their early twenties and a teenage son, all of whom conspired to dress me up in the latest Nepali fashions in order to disguise my age, which to them was shocking. To be in my thirties and to be alone, without children, unmarried, working, and *still* studying in school! I couldn't possibly tell people I was thirty-two and working on a PhD. Better to tell people I was twenty-five, an English teacher, and curious enough about Nepali life and culture to write a book about it. And so, following along, I did tell people that for a while, and it worked out for all of us. They got to tell their friends about the young, independent American girl sent by their uncle from the States to document Nepali stories, and I got to keep my age and spinsterhood a secret. Traversing this line between ethnographic truths and fictions was part of this storyteller's learning and doing, of speaking with/to, of contamination as collaboration. The text that follows is meant to be an exercise in listening/telling as Trinh T. Minh-ha conceptualizes it, a speaking nearby. I reconsider transnational realities and practice listening back as an English teacher and literacy researcher yielding, not to the empirical truth of stories but to their power to evoke, enact, and affect a reframing of what it means to learn in and for resettlement.

Re-thinking Transnational Realities

Speaking with/to was never fully about making transparent transnational realities like date of birth, migration status, and language and literacy identity as much as it was about opening space for stories to be told the way women intended them to be told, as rife with ambiguity, ambivalence, and betrayal, as is the case with the truth of any matter. In all honesty, it was hard to say what was true and not true about women's lives in relation to their living-English stories.

Was it true that Suk Maya viewed English as anything other than a survival literacy? To me, it seems that she deeply regrets that she did not get a chance to go to school when she was younger and fears that English "will not come." But she remains cautiously hopeful that eventually she will be able to speak the language. She tells me, "English is for everything," especially for reading signs and not getting lost. These ideas about English are repeated throughout our conversations and were reinforced in her English class by her teachers through dialogue exercises on how to ask for directions and word lists connected to food, shopping, and kitchen items among other "survival literacies." Indeed, the connection between English and survival was pervasive. Not only Suk Maya but many of her peers too claimed that "English is for everything." By comparison, it was common to hear that Nepali was nothing special, only to be used for "saying things inside the house."

Or was it true that Kausila, like most women her age living in the camps, did not receive a formal education? According to her, it was not until, at the age of fifty, with grown children having moved out of the house and an unsupportive husband disappeared into the hills of Ilam, she finally got the chance to learn. Our conversations often touched on this point—"learning at this age is like the joys and sorrows of home, I want to learn but I'm too old to remember anything!"

But when I first spoke with Kausila at the Beldangi I Bhutanese Refugee Camp Spoken English Center in mid-January 2013, it was clear that she could read and write. In fact, at our first meeting at her home she brought out several books and papers documenting her literacy practice and love of reading, especially old classics, like the *Ramayana* and the *Mahabharat*. She told me that she had been living in exile in Nepal for over fifteen years. Though upbeat and socially active, serving as a community coordinator for the Bhutanese-run Camp Watch Team, a kind of grassroots policing unit within the camp, and making regular appearances at the Spoken English Center, she was struggling to manage an unwieldy family situation that threatened her resettlement process with UNHCR and IOM. She spoke in hushed tones about her adult daughter's children running loose in the camps, about how her daughter's marriage to a local put the entire family's resettlement case on hold, about her hopes and fears related to these circumstances.

"The reason I study English," she says, "is when I go abroad everything will be in English.

"If we go there and ask anything in Nepali, they do not understand, but if we study English . . . well, if we come to Nepal and know Nepali is it very good. Like that, if we go abroad, we need English. That is why. Nepali doesn't work. That is why I study English.

"Another thing . . . " she says. "I was interested to learn when I was young and now after getting a chance to study, I will go to the foreign country where English is best and needed.

"English is the main thing saying like that, by knowing or not knowing, I have learning English. That is the reason. Though I have many problems at my house, if I say I have problems at my house, I will not get time. But then also I make time and go to class.

"I feel it is important. English means wherever we go we can speak. Nepali means only within Nepal. I feel it is useful, isn't it?"

On several occasions during our interviews together Kausila said that she was interested in learning and going to school when she was young but did not get the chance. Now she is taking advantage of every opportunity to learn, even though, as she says, "Now my eyes are weak, and my hand quivers when I write."

Kausila describes the duality of her present situation as a house full of both happiness and grief. She is happy to have the opportunity to learn at this age, but she is also grieving for what has been lost in the chaos brought on by protracted migration, according to her: her eyesight, her acuity, her youth. Now that the opportunity to learn is available to her, learning is made difficult by physical ailments brought on by aging.

Kausila's narrative speaks to the yearning and desiring to learn how to read and write, as if these skills had been denied to her all along. And knowing English is not just to repeat words in exchange for survival needs but to remember words, know them, and use them with intention. But was any of this yearning and desiring true? Did Kausila really desire these things? Did it really matter? Perhaps what mattered most to Kausila was making her narrative fit into a collective one rather than to stand out from the rest.

Susmita, Kali Maya, and Abi Maya all seemed to be navigating the gendered politics of language, literacy, and learning in relation to aging in resettlement:

"I didn't get a chance to read at the time [of Oxfam]," says Susmita, "because my children were very small. I didn't get time to go to school and now I'm regretting a lot. But what can I do? I am getting old. My mind is not working."

For Kali Maya, learning to read and write now is a matter of integrity, independence, or "to be able to stand on our own legs," as she puts it.

All are encouraged by the gradual progress they seem to be making in attending English classes at the Spoken English Center every day.

Susmita says, "I didn't know anything before. I did not even know how to write my name. Now I can make a signature and write my name . . . ."

Like many of the women I spoke with at the Spoken English Centers, the focal participants of this book spoke about how learning to write their names and produce signatures on important documents was a major lifetime accomplishment. They spoke of their struggles, now, to learn how to read and write the names of their children. They said that they believed that continued literacy development in English would be important to their resettlement process, and they all remarked on how their friends who had already resettled beseeched them to learn English and then come along to those distant places. But they also spoke about how hard it was to learn English, especially reading and writing. They spoke about learning how to get by with only "sign language" enough to "put rice in their mouths," as Suk Maya bluntly exclaims. But what about the desire for more than survival English? Beyond "putting rice in their mouths," what about English for integration, companionship, friendship, acceptance, and belonging?

"We will not be able to do anything in the US without English," is a repeated refrain among them. "Even the young ones will grow up not knowing Nepali at all." The women's stories collected here illustrate how older learners, with limited primary schooling, who have not been able to read or write for most of their adult lives, struggle with complicated, and at times, contradictory investments in learning to become readers and writers of a language that is not their first.

Ambivalence and ambiguity toward literacy development manifested themselves in a number of ways through interviews with women in the SECs. Many times, women linked their ambivalence to age and to biological aging processes that they claimed made it difficult for them to learn how to read or write. Suk Maya was fifty-two years old at the time of our interview. Like so many women I had spoken with, she, too, was a field hand in Bhutan, self-identified as "illiterate"; not able to provide a signature on documents certifying her family's rations in the camps, she routinely signed documents with a thumbprint only. Her resettlement process was underway, and she was anxiously waiting for her resettlement date to be called by the IOM, but she also feared that there might be some problem with her case that would stall her departure. She had been waiting, uncertainly, for months and taking English classes to pass the time. Suk Maya was skeptical of the value of those classes. In a follow-up interview to our initial meeting, she confided in me, "Education is important but what to do? The sense doesn't come, *bud'dhi āundaina*. Wisdom doesn't come to me. The mind is old. It is the time for us to die, though I'm interested to learn. If I had studied earlier . . . but I didn't know at that time."

Older learners, like Suk Maya, who spoke about their late-life literacy struggles seemed to offer me unique insights into life-wide and life-deep experiences of reading and writing and also what it meant to compose and perform literacy outside of formal school contexts and at the end of the life cycle.

Still, Susmita, Suk Maya, Kausila, Kali Maya, and Abi Maya were all fiercely focused on taking advantage of the refugee resettlement process's imperative to learn English. Their histories begin from early childhood and young adulthood with memories of education, work, and family in Bhutan, progressing through stories of their displacement and impending resettlements and their present-day hopes for learning English. Their stories illustrated to me both the commonalities and differences across their stated goals and motivations for learning. Also, through these stories, I came to find that despite their ambivalent attitudes toward learning English after a certain age, each woman persisted in attending classes at the Spoken English Centers. For them, English maintained a central place in their daily lives and visions for the future. Although it isn't clear the extent to which each woman was invested in becoming fluent, they all seemed to share a similar purpose in negotiating the cultural norms that informed their roles as daughters, wives, mothers, and grandmothers with the desire to learn. Their individual narratives, whether true or not, testify to the greater, collective struggle of an older generation of Bhutanese refugees caught between their memories of the past and uncertain futures.

Listening Back

Listening back, I recall these narrative encounters with women and what they teach me about storied experience as knowledge work. Stories of experience offer more than descriptive evidence of literacy practices. They are the product of situated narrative encounters, of a co-performance among listeners/tellers that evokes, enacts, and affects presences and absences. The women's stories of experience (re)told here point to the vicissitudes of transnational life and of shifting identifications with literacy across the lifespans of individuals in diaspora. In their evocations, women reclaim their desire for learning English, by placing emphasis on the absences and presences, the mobilities and (im)mobilities of their literate histories and resources across migration pathways.

Susmita, Suk Maya, Kali Maya, Abi Maya, and Kausila *evoke* the gendered and sexual dimensions of the absence of literacy in their stories by pointing to the ways in which they were denied literacy education in early childhood by their parents. Suk Maya and Susmita evoke their experience of the absence of literacy through their speaking, their word work with me. Using the language and narrative strategies at our disposal, Suk Maya and Susmita respond creatively to the tensions and contradictions of resettlement by calling our attention to a present absence—the materially structured and ideological denial of literacy that they have experienced as individuals throughout their lives and the contextualization of their personal struggles within a larger community consciousness about the value of literacy later in life. Kali Maya participates in storytelling that is a remembering, reprocessing, and reinterpreting of the absence of literacy in a collective context. In her story, Kali Maya forges a connection between her memories of being denied literacy education early in life and the decision she has made later in life to go to school, claiming an empowered, gendered subjecthood as an educated person who is identified with and engaged in literacy learning as oppositional struggle, to become literate "so as not to be suppressed by our sons and grandsons."

In addition to evoking absence, women *enact* a "theory in the flesh," or what Cherríe Moraga and Gloria Anzaldúa have described as a "politic born out of necessity," out of the embodied and relational experience of living, learning, loving (19). Kausila, through her experience-oriented stories, describes great feats of strength and sacrifice she performed to ensure her children could go to school in Bhutan. And during her protracted displacement in Nepal, Kausila describes performing a nonliterate identity (it's not clear to what extent Kausila might be considered literate in reading and writing) so as not to be passed up for women's learning opportunities offered by an NGO-sponsored literacy program in the early years of the displacement. In Chapter 4, Abi Maya's performance of "being lost" in the jungle, enacted through a metanarrative about "a hungry shepherd" who fails to write a letter home that will ensure his survival, plays with the framing of identities-in-motion by pointing to ideological contradictions within the place, space, and time of resettlement.

Susmita, Suk Maya, and Kali Maya are all adult language learners seeking to prepare themselves for life after resettlement. But their vision of the future is uncertain, and their memories of the past are in tension with their desire to learn in the present. In their stories of learning, women enact this contradiction through relationships to literacy that are deeply kinetic, a movement bound to and beyond the history of their nonliteracy and their identifications with nonliteracy. Indeed, women continue to inhabit a nonliterate subjectivity, even as they devote six hours a day, five days a week to learning how to read and write, coming and going from their homes to the language centers. Women's representations of themselves as nonliterate in their stories of learning complicates and interrupts easy assumptions about women's agency in relationship to their investments in learning English. Far from an insular or narrow local literacy practice resistant to the global imperatives of a widely circulating literacy myth, women's simultaneous desire and refusal to adopt the position of a "literate subject" works as an intervention in and negotiation of their literacy experience within a realm of possibility that women explore through their acts of learning.

Indeed, all these women *affect* or put into affect shifting identities, nonliterate and literate, while claiming new, empowered subject positions. They are women who were previously denied literacy but who now, later in life, choose, themselves, to go to school. Their stories unfold within the margins between these identities and subject positions and within the performative, threshold spaces of the learning contexts of their transnational migration. Writing matters. It matters to Susmita, Suk Maya, and Kali Maya. But not for the reasons I originally thought. Platitudes like "writing matters" elide how histories of the movement of people and their literacy practices, including the gendered and sexed practices of denying women early and secondary forms of education, have come to shape the "mattering" of writing and of literacy in the lived experience of others. As literacy scholars have argued, the denial of literacy is itself an act of literacy, that when evoked can point to systemic inequalities and histories of exclusion (Branch, "What No Literacy Means").

Women evoke, enact, and affect literacy learning in their stories, circling around local-global tensions, connecting past, present, and future, and not wholly submitting to literacy's accumulations or forward movement. Picking up on these tensions, particularly through the themes of presence, absence, and sensuous coalition, the second part of this book is a resiting of these stories in and through a series of snapshots, time lapses, and analysis. However, in this second part, I invite readers into a mode of analysis that is not wholly straightforward. Each chapter begins with two snapshots, detailing scenes of learning taking place on either side of the resettlement process in the United States and Nepal.

Following each of the snapshots is some contextualization of the scenes followed by a "time lapse." In digital photography and documentary filmmaking, time lapses describe a sequence of frames that record active and transformative processes over a long period of time. When the frames are shown together quickly, the effect is to make the action speed up, lending emphasis to the change that occurs. I use the metaphor of snapshots and time lapses to structure the ethnographic narratives that follow, partly to emphasize the temporal dimensions of learning in and for migration, but also those of speaking with/to. I pause in the lapse in time between frames to disrupt the chronology of ethnographic representations of migration and to engage in critical reflexiveness. In this space between pre- and post-resettlement scenes, I return to the stories of the first part of the book and continue to be in dialogue with them in relation to the layering of meaning produced by the snapshots and their contextualization.

In this space between, I am "learning to learn" from women's stories, situating them across languages, locations, and time, approaching them not as a distanced, expert witness, but as someone who has been moved by stories to sit uncomfortably in an intermediate stage of (im)possible knowing, responding to stories that are not mine to fully know or claim.

PART II
LEARNING TO LEARN: SITUATING STORIES ACROSS LANGUAGES, LOCATIONS, AND TIME

Part II

Learning to Learn: Situating Stories across Languages, Locations, and Time

THE CHAPTERS IN THE SECOND PART OF this book explore the meanings of transnational literacy learning that emerge from the stories women tell in Part I. Specifically, I attend to the central themes of absence and nonliteracy (Chapter 7) and the forms of sensuous coalition women enact in relationship to these themes (Chapter 8). In attending to these themes and outcomes, I return to women's stories and the meanings and effects women evoke in them. Moving back and forth across contexts of learning, I reflect on women's evocations of absence and enactments of coalition *before* resettlement. I put these reflections into conversation with my encounters with the stories of women who are navigating the tensions and contradictions of English-only language and literacy education *after* resettlement.

This movement allows for the critical work of *learning to learn*, or the "slow, attentive, mind-changing (on both sides) ethical singularity" that Spivak writes about in her afterword to *Imaginary Maps: Three Stories by Mahasweta Devi*, a work of literary translation (200-201). It is, as Spivak writes elsewhere, a "setting-to-work" with others across distances in time and location ("Responsibility"). Similarly, in my dialogues with women on either side of the refugee resettlement process, I am "learning to learn" on their terms but never wholly outside of the contaminated space of the dislocations and relocations reinscribed through the uneven power dynamics of our collaborative endeavors around their language and literacy education.

Moving back and forth across contexts of learning, I reflect on women's evocations of literacy absence as enactments of coalition, and, in doing so, I develop my own moving literacies that intersect women's moving literacies and practices. Through ethnographic narrative, I weave snapshots of pre- and post-resettlement language and literacy investments into dialogue with critical reflections that occur in the elapsed space and time between the snapshots. The chapters in Part II are thus organized through a listening/(re)telling praxis that emerges in the compression and expansion of space and time in an ethnographic narrative, where stories and storytellers move back and forth across languages and sites of learning.

In Chapter 7, "*Hāttī PaDhēra Thulō Hudaina* / 'Elephants Don't Get Big by Reading': Literacy Presence from Stories of Absence across Resettlement Locations," I consider how women's evocations of literacy denial as an absent presence inform their daily learning practices and might be used to recast our theoretical frameworks for others' investments in and desire for literacy. This chapter reflects on women's insistence on their nonliteracy despite their being fully immersed in literate settings and the ways in which their intersubjective and lived experience of literacy learning does not necessarily conform to conventional framings of literacy development as accumulation or of the desire for literacy as a precondition for inhabiting agency.

In Chapter 8, "*Hāmī Khēlchaū Sangīnī* / 'We Sing and Dance a *Sangīnī*': Literacies on the Move and in Sensuous Coalition," I begin with a description of a seasonal song and dance that is performed at a Spoken English Center closing ceremony to ask how women on the brink of resettlement negotiate multiple, conflicting desires related to language, learning, and love through learning as a performance of friendship and solidarity formed in diasporic community.

In Chapter 9, "Conclusion: Between Novice and Expert— Living English, Moving Literacies" I offer a conclusion to the book that summarizes listening to/(re)telling stories as dialogic praxis and points to the implications for future research that goes beyond voicing differences to enacting transformative co-inquiry.

Exploring transnational literacy learning this way, I move back and forth across situational contexts and stories of experience that emerge through the refugee resettlement process. In this liminal space between the United States and Nepal, transnational literacy becomes a way of navigating different epistemic frameworks and other viewpoints. Transnational literacy learning means learning to learn from others' moving literacies, the ones they harness to be in and move through a chaotic world. Learning to learn means "setting to work" with others beyond a sense of responsibility for their survival. Instead, learning to learn responds to a call *to* ethics from others, shifting responsibility *for* others to a responsibility *to* figuring out how to flourish together in the ruins left behind by displacement and expulsion.

For Spivak, *setting to work* is an engagement in an (im)possible ethics, which is not to say that ethics are impossible but that ethical encounters with others are impossible to replicate because of the complexities of the contexts in which these engagements unfold. Thus, our relationships with others must be approached with tenacity, commitment, and singularity, Spivak says, "with love" ("Afterword" 200). Again, setting to work means learning to learn from others how to be responsible *to* each other versus *for* each other. I do not tell women's stories because they cannot. I tell women's stories as part of their call to me to listen and retell them.

7. HĀTTĪ PADHĒRA THULŌ HUDAINA /"ELEPHANTS DON'T GET BIG BY READING": LITERACY PRESENCE FROM STORIES OF ABSENCE ACROSS RESETTLEMENT LOCATIONS

They say we didn't study when we were young. Why should we read now? They say that we should educate our sons and daughters, but why should we go in our old age? If we suggest to them that we will be able to learn a few things here at the Spoken English Center, they reply:

"Why to go there? We have much work!"
They say many things. "Elephants don't get big by reading!"
They say this, and, also, "Why should the people whose teeth have ripened go to school?"
        —Women's Group Interview, Beldangi I, January 2013

Snapshot: Two Families, Three Generations, Learning English
In an apartment complex on the east side of Tucson, June 2012

When she was sixty-nine years old, Januka's main reason for attending English class every day, Monday through Friday, for hours at a time, was "for the purposes of understanding." She expresses surprise at how quickly her youngest grandchildren in Texas had learned to speak English.

When I ask her how her grandchildren are doing, she says, "They know so much English but only a very little Nepali!"

The language and generation gap seemed to startle and fascinate her.

Januka is studying, also, to become a citizen, though she remains unconvinced as to whether or not she would be able to pass the citizenship test.

"I will try," she says to me.

"But I don't have the knowledge."

"*Ke garne?*" she says, "what to do?"

Sabitra, Januka's daughter-in-law, is in her late forties at the time that I was close with the family, from around 2008 to 2012, in the early days of the resettlement process. Sabitra attends three sets of classes: a Tucson International Alliance of Refugee Communities (TIARC) citizenship classes four days a week, a refugee-led, bilingual citizenship class on Thursday evenings, and a Pima Community College class, also four days a week. Sabitra was employed on and off during the early days of her resettlement, but the employment wasn't going well. Ambika, Sabitra's twenty-something daughter, and I speak about it in their living room one afternoon sipping warm, sweet milk tea together.

Ambika explains that Sabitra had originally gotten a job as a housekeeper in an upscale hotel, which had her working long hours, sometimes ten-hour days, six days a week. This was Sabitra's first job ever, and she was exhausted. She stopped going to class, not because she didn't want to learn English, but because she was so tired. Still, there was a desire to know English so she could understand what people were saying to her at work. For instance, as part of her job, Sabitra would sometimes get tips. The tips were put in envelopes marked "to" and "from" and sometimes the guests would leave messages for her. Ambika remembers her mom bringing the envelopes and messages home and wanting to know what they said. Translating for her mom, Ambika explains that Sabitra wanted to know English so that could read the messages guests left for her and be able to make a connection in that way. The job didn't last long; Sabitra couldn't keep up with the long hours being on her feet. So, she left that job to focus on her English. When Sabitra wasn't in English class, she would drive to the Department of Economic Security office to turn in proof of her class attendance, which would earn her fifty dollars a month to go toward bus passes.

When I ask Sabitra what she was doing in her classes, she goes to retrieve her class folder so that she could show me her work. In her folder were several worksheets with illustrated spelling exercises, matching pairs, and singular and plural practice. Having taught Sabitra in my own classes for several years, I have imagined that her English would have progressed far beyond the work she had completed in the worksheets. Yet even in our friendly and informal conversations over tea, Ambika did most of the translating and talking.

Indeed, I had the same sense of Januka's progress as well. Despite very strong investments in learning to read and write in English, it seemed that both she and Sabitra were to be perpetually stuck in preliterate classes, positioned by their teachers and other literacy workers as "unable to even hold a pencil." Januka, for example, despite going to class five days a week for over three years, never progressed beyond perfunctory greetings and short phrases in English.

When I ask Januka about her goals for learning, she said:

"I want to understand and be able to know how to talk and say things, like vegetables. I want to know the word for *potato* in English.

"And I want to know English for the purposes of understanding what other people say."

Januka's weekly schedule of English classes was strenuous, including a two-hour English language training program she attended on the east side of town Monday through Thursday as well as citizenship classes offered through a local library and community center on Monday, Wednesday, and Thursday evenings. She also sometimes attended an afternoon class on Tuesday and Thursday run at an elementary school located close to her home and would occasionally stop by a class I taught on Saturday mornings at the TIARC learning center.

Januka keeps a red work folder where she saved worksheets, exercises, and an odd assortment of handouts she collected in each of her classes, including a K–1 Reader Readiness workbook. She had scrawled her name across the front of the folder in big black letters made with a marker. Her name was also written upside down in blue ink on the back bottom part of the folder. Her work folder contained several handouts, a map of the United States, and a brochure from TIARC. The handouts were out of order and incomplete. They mostly consisted of letter tracing exercises and pre-alphabet practice. Several of the letter exercises were out of order, with letter sequences missing. Other handouts include packets of number tracing exercises and a fill-in-the-blank calendar.

In an apartment just underneath Januka's, I meet with twenty-seven-year-old Pabi, the daughter-in-law of Januka's close friend Mon Maya, a woman in her late seventies who wasn't attending English classes or any classes, for that matter. On the wall by the door to the apartment there were collages of family and deities from Nepal. Pabi motions me toward the collages, pointing out her sister and mother, who are still in the camps. On the opposite wall there were four pieces of white construction paper; on each of the papers was a letter in English—A, B, C. Pabi explains that she was using the papers to teach her three-year-old, Darshan, the alphabet.

Mon Maya joins us. She sits at a distance on what looked like a hand-me-down futon pushed back on the far wall of the living area by the hallway to the back bedrooms. She has long white hair that she pulled back into a low ponytail. She wears a pink short-sleeved mini-cardigan with a gold-and-burgundy wrap skirt. She also wears a green marriage necklace and a tika.

Pabi chats almost nonstop in the most fluent English, a soft lilt to her voice. She was an English teacher in the camps. She pulls out boxes of textbooks and certificates. English grammar manuals, vocabulary exercises. She tells me I should look out for the headmaster of her school when I go to Nepal and scribbles his address in my notebook.

I'm curious about Mon Maya, who watches all of this intently from the futon but doesn't say a word. I ask Pabi if she wouldn't mind translating for me so that I might ask Mon Maya a few questions about her life pre-resettlement, her goals for her life now. Pabi translates.

Mon Maya recalls living in a large three-story house in Bhutan with more than a dozen family members. They had farm animals to take care of, fields to sow and harvest. She wasn't educated, there was no time for that. And after, when the family was forced out of their home and crossed into Nepal to live in the camps, she wasn't interested in studying. She liked to sew and cook and take care of the house, and that's what she did for nearly twenty years while she lived in the camps.

When I ask Mon Maya if she had any intentions of learning English now, for conversation at home with Darshan or to go for citizenship, she laughed. "I've been like this all my life! Why should I learn now?" But she thought about it and added that it was very important for women like her daughter-in-law to learn. "They should go to school," she says, "and the future will be very bright for the Nepali-speaking Bhutanese growing up in the US."

Snapshot: "Elephants Don't Get Big by Reading" (Nepal)
At the edge of the jungle along the Maidhar River in Jhapa, January 2013

It is a sunny Tuesday morning in Magh, the tenth lunar month of the Bikram Sambat, the official Nepali calendar. The Bhutanese refugee camp at Beldangi in Jhapa district, Nepal, is coiled up in the tendrils of freshly sprouted green onions, and the delicate yellow blossoms of mustard-seed plants ripple like lace on the current of a tranquil breeze. Ripened sugar apples from high up in the jungle canopy drop to the forest floor, exploding fruit bombs that ooze a cream-colored custard from cracked green scales. Emptied shells are scattered about my path.

I've been coming to the Beldangi Spoken English Center almost every morning for five months to attend the English teacher's daily planning meetings and to talk with the adult learners about their resettlement stories. As he does every morning, Thalu, the center guard, greets me in the clearing behind the center's massive swinging gate, hinged to a bamboo fence that runs the perimeter of the classrooms. He offers me spiced milk tea and then begins setting up in an open square shape the colorful woven mats we will use for our morning focus group. By the time I arrive, the English lessons are already taking shape around the day's topic—going places. I hear Manju's strong, syncopated voice leading learners in a recitation of a dialogue about how to get to the hospital, by foot, by car, by bus.

Classes like this have been in session since the start of the resettlement process before 2007, but as resettlement gains momentum and more and more people leave the camps every day, interest in English class is waning. These days, the focus has turned to "date waiting"—holding on with bated breath for the end of an indefinite period of time from the approval of a resettlement case to the announcement of the date of departure. After over two decades of displacement, it is difficult for people in the camps to concentrate on anything other than resettlement.

Geeta, a former center facilitator called an "in-charge," arrives with eight focus group participants, all women, whose ages range from twenty-seven to fifty. We get settled on the woven mats and begin.

"Okay, we'll start," says Geeta in English, then switching over into Nepali she describes the focus-group scenario.

Geeta and I have been planning for the focus group to be about the attendance issues the center is currently facing. Recently, there has been some pressure put on center staff to recruit more learners to the center. With dwindling numbers, it is difficult to tell how long the sponsoring agency will be able to incentivize instruction through teacher stipends. Teachers and learners at the center have been participating in community outreach, visiting neighbors and friends to persuade them to join classes, but for the most part these missions have done very little to garner interest in learning English. Teachers and learners are beginning to feel that the English classes are a lost cause.

Rather than dwell on this sad fact, Geeta and I thought it might work best to encourage focus-group participants to engage in a discussion of the possible reasons community members had for not joining the classes by imagining what they were doing instead. It was a kind of research experiment we had concocted after a couple of more pointed interviews had fallen flat.

Still, the scenario we had dreamed up feels awkward. It takes some prodding for the focus-group participants to warm up to the idea. At first, no one in the focus group will speak up. There are some nervous giggles, and Geeta looks at me, perplexed. I shrug my shoulders in an exaggerated way and look around. Geeta tries again.

"At this time, what are people doing instead of coming to class? Think of all the things they are doing! Use your imagination! What do you see them doing on your way to class?" she says.

Finally, Puspa, a woman in her twenties and the youngest focus-group member, begins with her recollection of meeting another woman, Nor Maya, on the way to class. According to Puspa, she had asked Nor Maya why she wasn't coming to class, and Nor Maya had ignored her.

"I met Nor Maya on the way," says Puspa. "And I asked her, why didn't you come to school? Why are you not coming? In your absence school is dark. You will forget what you learned before. She said, 'Puspa, I am busy. I don't get time these days. Later, I will come.'"

"Why do you think women like Nor Maya are not coming here?" Geeta asks Puspa.

"Maybe they are not coming here because they feel shy. That's what I think," says Puspa. "They say, 'How can I study if I don't know how to read? I will feel embarrassed. Everyone will laugh at me!' That is why they are not coming, because of shyness and they don't come because they don't make the time."

Turning to engage the woman sitting next to Puspa, Geeta says, "Auntie, on the way to school what do you see?"

"What is there to say? I don't know," Naina Maya sighs with exasperation.

Then she says slyly, "People cutting chickens!"

The group giggles, but the ice is finally broken. Then everyone begins sharing their observations. The group describes people walking along the path, coming and going, running their errands, accomplishing some tasks at the nearby medical clinic, and gossiping with neighbors.

Then one woman says, "If you ask why they're not coming to the Spoken English Center, they'll tell you it's because we are grown up like this since our birth. We didn't go to school and we're okay. Why should we go now? 'Why should we go there!?' they insist."

"It's true," says another woman. "Many people are talking like that. 'I won't go,' they say. 'If I repeat a word ten times at that language center, I still won't remember it! People will laugh at me,' they say. Many people are saying, 'We'll learn only after going to America.'

"Also, I have many friends who have registered for English classes, but they are not coming. In this class, I have a neighbor like that. My neighbor doesn't like to come. Others say, 'I don't know anything! I don't know how to write! I haven't studied before!' What can I say to them, right? I try to tell them that it will be easier for them in the US if they learn to read and write here, but they refuse to come, and they say it isn't necessary to study here. Whether that is true or not, I don't know. I only know what they tell me."

Geeta asks for some clarification. "So you are saying that people are lazy, and that is the reason they aren't coming to school, or are there other reasons?"

"I don't know," another participant says. "They don't know anything, and they think their friends will laugh at them. What is there to do? They are full of regret!"

"Also, what work is there to do in the camps? There is no reason not to study," says another.

"That's right! Mostly, on our way to class, we see people sitting and talking, playing cards and sitting. There is no other work for people besides that, and the ladies simply sit and talk about others. Nothing else."

"Why is that?" asks Geeta.

Imagining what must be going through the minds of the ones who do not come, one participant says, "'We didn't study when we were young. Why should we read now?' They say that we should educate our sons and daughters, but why should we go in our old age? If we suggest to them that we will be able to learn a few things here, they reply, 'Why to go there? We have much work!' They say many things. 'Elephants don't get big by reading!' They say this.

"Why should the people's whose teeth have ripened go to school?"

The snapshots above depict how women, in their evocations of absence, channel the desire for literacy and for English into a re-narrating and re-forming of multiple and shifting identities—literate and nonliterate—across migration pathways. Literacy learning later in life in the context of recent resettlement, rather than remaking women's lives and identities as literate, multilingual migrants who are fluent in English-Nepali crossings, is an opportunity, instead, for these women to contest the literacy myth through their experience of absence—to make visible the elephant in the room, to voice the silence of a silencing absence. Literacy-learning events and practices are catalysts for these women making present the absence of literacy and connecting this absence to their experiencing of its hope and violence in their unsettled present and imagined futures.

In the first snapshot, "Two Families, Three Generations, Learning English," for example, women's goals for learning come into friction with the historical absence of literacy education in women's lives. Sabitra grapples with literacy learning in this way at her housekeeping job at a hotel when she relays her experience of interacting with hotel guests through tip envelopes and messages that guests leave behind. Sabitra receives notes from hotel guests that she cannot read; she brings these back to her daughter, who reads them for her. Sabitra struggles with the desire to be able to read these herself and is understandably frustrated that several years of English lessons have not enabled her to understand even the simplest of messages. Sabitra's story makes clear the unevenness of learning and acquiring language and literacy, that literacy skills are not uniformly acquired nor do they accumulate in linear fashion.

Januka, Sabitra's mother-in-law, also has goals for learning and for literacy and attends class daily for hours at a time with little to show for her efforts. She has acquired a few words for kitchen items and is able to scrawl her name, but she continues to feel the frustration of not being able to grasp the language as quickly as do her grandchildren. She expresses a sense of dismay at being left behind. Mon Maya, too, is clear about her relationship to absence when she says, "I never learned when I was young, why should I learn now!" It's an intergenerational claim and a standpoint from which she relates to the language and literacy investments of her daughter-in-law and grandson. Each of these examples speaks to the absence of literacy as a literacy act that both works *on* women, shaping their relationships to family, work, and outsiders, and is also worked *by* women. When Mon Maya lays claim to that history of absence as an integral part of who she is in relation to her family, she is agentively working the absence of literacy as an act of literacy that invites her listener to consider the lifelong and intergenerational impact of that absence.

In the second snapshot, "Elephants Don't Get Big by Reading," women grapple with recruiting efforts to draw more women to the language centers and the way these efforts are often met with indignation from women in their local sectors. "Elephants don't get big by reading" is a phrase that results in both laughter and chagrin. The women who attend classes consider such a phrase to signal the ignorance of an uneducated, vernacular worldview. The dynamic that is created is one of us versus them—the ones who attend English classes versus the ones who don't. Yet even among the women who do invest in learning English, there is skepticism around literacy outcomes and whether or not learning a new language is even possible after a certain age. There is joy in coming together, but also hardship in the physical, social, and cognitive constraints of learning later in life in the context of a protracted displacement.

The absence of literacy is a profoundly layered historical and political phenomenon affecting women in the camps. Acknowledging that absence is an act of a deeply moving literacy—a performance and rhetoric of possibilities—that moves recursively and recalcitrantly between empowerment and critique of literacy hope and the violence of literacy. Women use the absence of literacy to make claims about the power and virtuousness of literacy learning as well as to interrupt outsiders' organized efforts to direct English-medium literacy campaigns for adults.

Time Lapse: Literacy Stories as Stories of Absence

In order to contextualize and theorize the snapshots above through the lens of women's stories, I think back to my storytelling encounters in Part I, and especially to Abi Maya. There was a moment in my conversations with Abi Maya that helps me elucidate the significance of the absence of literacy in women's lives before resettlement: the story of the hungry shepherd.

As I mentioned earlier, there was a saying among the older learners in the Bhutanese refugee camps, *Go Thalā bhōkalā māralā*, which roughly translates as "The hungry shepherd died." As Abi Maya recounts it, it refers to a story about an old shepherd who goes into the forest with a herd of cattle for several months out of the year, a not-uncommon practice among the people of the eastern hills of Nepal, a people that many of the Bhutanese refugees trace their lineage to through their history of migration from this region to Bhutan in the early part of the twentieth century. The story goes that the shepherd was beginning to run out of rice when a passerby crosses his path. Desperate to send word to his family to please send rice the shepherd has the passerby convey a message to the family. But, just as in a game of telephone, the message that is eventually conveyed to the family is not the message that the shepherd intended. Instead of receiving word that the shepherd is starving and needs rice to be sent, the family receives the message that the shepherd has died of starvation and no rice should be sent. The older learners in the refugee camp English centers repeated the phrase often and usually with great humor as an example of feeling "lost in translation" or not being able to fully express their thought or meaning through language.

One moral to be taken from the story is that having language or being literate doesn't save lives; you can't depend on it for survival. Reinforcing the power of the epithet, the proverb is never unpacked. Simply saying *"Go Thalā bhōkalā mārala"* is enough to invoke its larger context and lots of affable laughter. Older learners deploy the proverb as both a pithy saying to describe themselves, emphatically, as uneducated and also as a parable about the limits and consequences of (il)literacy. The saying elicits knowing laughter from peers and looks of bewilderment from members of a younger generation. When I came to this segment of conversation in my story recordings with my research assistant in Nepal, Shankar, he stopped the recording and laughed. "This is funny," he said. "It's like an old way of speaking." He spelled out the proverb for me as I transcribed it into my field notes and then carefully explained to me the story behind the reference. When I brought the phrase back with me to Tucson, Arizona, I asked the family of two of my oldest students, Januka, to whom I refer in the snapshot above, and her husband Kamal, both in their seventies, if they could help give me some more context for the proverb. Januka and Kamal's granddaughter, a fluent English speaker in her early twenties, puzzled over it. "I don't know what it means," she said with a shrug. But Kamal knew, and he laughed and laughed and asked me to repeat it over and over again in my rudimentary Nepali. He eventually wrote it out for me in Devanagari script in the ratty corner of an old notebook I carried with me on all my interviews and house calls. The notebook has since been lost. But when I think about the phrase now, I hear it clearly in my mind. I hear Kamal's long, hearty laughter. I think about the women in that focus group in Nepal. *"Go Thalā bhōkalā mārala,"* they would chide each other ruefully. "We are just like that old shepherd!"

Abi Maya is not the only woman to evoke the absence of literacy and the experience of absence in this way. Susmita evokes the absence of literacy in all of our conversations. It's pervasive. That history never leaves her. It's part of her story, part of her value system. Her other beliefs about English include the role of English as a prestige language, a language that is clearly more important than Nepali in the United States. Her highest aim is to learn just enough English to be able to write her name. She also mentions feeling a lot of pressure to find a job after resettlement since she will not be old enough to receive Social Security insurance. This pressure is compounded by the idea that she "will not be able to do anything in the US" without English. She believes that older people should learn English because there is nothing else for them to do in the camp. According to her, Nepali is a useless language; everyone she knows who has left the camp will be speaking English in the US. Even the young ones will grow up not knowing Nepali at all.

Like some others who have resettled, she envisions using body language, rather than the spoken word, to communicate in English in the United States. She hopes to be able to read sign boards and vehicle and house numbers one day. Based on what she has heard from people who have resettled, she feels that she will learn the language "as per the place" and likens herself and her struggle with the language to me since I am trying to speak Nepali while in Nepal but did not know Nepali well before I came to the place. In the excerpt below, she talks about her struggle to acquire English in the camp and what she imagines it will be like to use the language after resettlement.

As Susmita tries to negotiate the language-learning imperative of resettlement, she is caught between cultural frames in transnationalism. First, there is her cultural frame for learning related to age, gender, and family. She says, "I didn't get a chance to read at the time [of Oxfam] because my children were very small. I didn't get time to go to school, and now I'm regretting a lot. But what can I do? I am getting old. My mind is not working." Second, there is the disruption caused by the resettlement process wherein she sees people from her sector leaving studying English, leaving the camp, and then reporting back that communicating without English abroad is like "beating around the bush." However, far from being paralyzed by the disruption of migration and language shift, Susmita is shrewd and self-aware as she tracks the gradual progress she makes with literacy.

She says, "I didn't know anything before. I did not even know how to write my name. Now I can make a signature and write my name."

The theme of name writing comes up several times throughout the interview, but it's a point that Susmita always qualifies.

She says, "Now I can make a signature and write my name, but I do not know how to write others' names. I have learned only that much education here."

While she is clearly proud of her new capacity for writing, she is quick to comment that she has only acquired a very truncated form of literacy.

Throughout our conversations, Susmita shuffles between a deeper sense that literacy is for "clever" people, like her friend who studied in the Spoken English Centers and left three or four years ago, but does not come easily to the people who have been left behind in the camp, people who are uneducated and have some problems with their resettlement process. On several occasions, Susmita says clearly that she is learning English just enough to name some objects, but she is uncertain about learning to read and write.

She says, "The reason for learning English is for us to go abroad. If we don't know English, we are not able to do anything there. That is why English is important. Without it, nothing is possible, I think, so I am learning.

"Mostly, [English] is not coming to me, but I know the names of a few things like fruit and vegetables, kitchen items.

"If I know such things, they [English speakers] will be able to understand me. For this [knowledge] only I am studying.

"I am learning [to use English] by mouth.

"I cannot write by my hand.

"I am getting old and my hand, it shakes."

Susmita, like many of the women I spoke with at the Spoken English Centers, felt that learning how to write her name and produce a signature on important documents were both major lifetime accomplishments. She struggles now to learn how to read and write the names of her children. But she believes that continued literacy development in English is important to her resettlement process, and she remarks on how their friends who have already resettled around the globe beg her to learn English and then come along to those distant places.

But Susmita also knows from being in conversation with those who have resettled that achieving language proficiency is a struggle and that many in the resettlement community get by with only "sign language" enough to "put rice in their mouth holes—*mukh bhaat*," as her friend, Suk Maya, crudely exclaims.

The pressure to learn English for more than survival—for integration, companionship, friendship, acceptance, belonging—is acute. As Susmita remarks, "We will not be able to do anything in the US without English!" Another fear is that of becoming increasingly obsolete and isolated in a new land, where even the children and grandchildren will be adopting new ways of living and speaking, primarily in English.

"Even the young ones," Susmita says, "will grow up not knowing Nepali at all."

Susmita's story illustrates how older learners, women in midlife and beyond with limited primary schooling, who have not been able to read or write for most of their adult lives, struggle with complicated and at times contradictory investments in learning to become readers and writers of a language that is not their first. Their gendered literacy histories reveal the way early, culturally patterned family roles, relationships, and obligations shaped their childhood literacy experiences and opportunities to learn, and continue to shape the ambivalences that characterize their tolerance for and struggle with English-language learning in the present.

Like Susmita, Suk Maya expresses trouble figuring out what to do with the letters she has learned in the Spoken English Center. There are practical reasons and personal reasons why she would want to come to class day after day, but her progress is slow, and every day in class she is reminded that learning to read and write is arduous. Literacy does not just come to her spontaneously; it is not something she can simply absorb by getting close to it in class. Yet in the midst of this struggle, Suk Maya attends English class daily with other women in order to get a chance to learn something before she dies. The act of going is school and learning from her teachers is sacred to Suk Maya in the way that a daughter's relationship to her parents is sacred in Nepali culture. She even likens her teachers to present-day parents, "true" parents, rather than duplicate ones. Her birth parents, she says, are duplicates of each other, and perhaps she means, duplicates of a cultural practice and time in which girls were not permitted to go to school but were sold into other families for "the price of one *tola* of gold and a pregnant cow."

Stories of absence reframe transnational literacies in motion by shifting the focus from a theory of the (im)mobility of resources in migration to the situated history of lived experience that becomes imprinted on the body and its movements across time and space. Abi Maya's traveling story of the hungry shepherd, Susmita's "weak eyes" and "shaking hands," Suk Maya's pregnant cow, invite us into new stories as they work to create another presence from the absence of literacy (Garcia "Creating").

At least a decade has passed since I first encountered Januka, Sabitra, and Mon Maya in that apartment complex in Tucson. Not long after this encounter, I met women on the other side of the resettlement process in refugee camps in Nepal who were gathering together to plan their recruitment strategy for the next batch of English classes despite widespread resistance to adult language and literacy learning among camp residents who scoff, "Elephants don't get big by reading." Looking back on these snapshots and listening to the audio fragments of focus groups I conducted during my research in Nepal, the voices from that protracted displacement reverberate as clear as day, cling to the moment and then dissipate like fine mist. I wonder if these women are still alive, where they are, what became of them. Did they ever learn to write their names in Nepali or in English? Or the names of their children?

Circling back to these stories now, I am struck by the way literacy learning conceptualized in vernacular ways of speaking, and through proverbs like that of the hungry shepherd, does not conform to conventional framings of literacy development as accumulation. Indeed, the story of the hungry shepherd seems to poke fun at the notion of literacy accumulation through an emphasis on its absence or the limitations of vernacular literacies in meeting the needs of the traveler, the migrant, the roaming shepherd. The shepherd goes hungry because his limited, local literacy skills fail him when he is farthest from his home and in his most dire hour.

Women's stories of absence reckon with tensions within experience and the kinds of agency, community, and consciousness that has been denied articulation by hegemonic discourse. Women's stories do not represent mere information about transnational literacy learning but prompt listeners to participate in imaginative space for reckoning with the contradictions of their accumulated literacy resources.

Stories also invite what María Lugones calls "loving perception," a kind of listening practice attuned to what it is a listener might least expect. When we read these texts as a creative response to globally situated tensions, then we confront the texts neither as representations nor as fictions but as invitations to reconsider the historical world from the perspective of those narratives. The texts become aids for thinking from the standpoints of others' lives; that is, interpreting the world in view of the insights of those who have struggled against oppression or exploitation.

These stories are less about representing transnational realities and more about actively navigating and negotiating ambivalence, connection, belonging, and the possibilities of re-storying literate identities (how women identify as either literate or nonliterate) and subjectivity (their relationship to literacy as subjects of my study and as agentive subjects engaged in language and literacy practices). Women's stories of the absence of literacy are stories that contend with the tensions and contradictions of their experience in diaspora—tensions and contradictions between the value of literacy learning according to the sponsors of their resettlement, and the way literacy and its valuing is lived on multiple levels; historically, socially, psychologically, and bodily. Women's narratives that reckon with these contradictions do not simply describe what is felt, lived, and perceived, transparently, but serve as creative forms for rearticulating and reconfiguring what is experienced. Through these narratives, women confront the lived tension and contradiction of literacy values in ways that make sense to them and allow them to navigate that incommensurability in the context of their forced dislocation and ongoing relocation.

Women's investments in literacy were never clear-cut, especially in their stories of experience. Rather, stories pointed to embodied, gendered, ideological meaning-making practices in which women's agency wasn't always clearly defined. The lack of clear definition around women's agency and its relationship to their language and literacy investments was difficult for me to make sense of in terms of rhetoric and composition's paradigmatic framing of literacy development as accumulation. In the literacy-as-accumulation model, literacy operates within an economy of literacy where the value of and hope associated with reading and writing is mythic, and people "take hold" of the literacy myth and its tangible resources to advance their personal goals. Accumulating literacies offers one theory of literate agency. The women's stories presented here are not to deny the significance of writing and of literacy in shaping people's worlds and opportunities but to make the case that different women and communities of women across the globe grapple with the myth and mandate of literacy, transnational literacy resources, and literacy's naturalized associations with English in different ways. Investments shift, change, move unevenly through migration processes and pathways. Women's stories provided a way of navigating the incommensurability of transnational literacy goals and values with women's literacy histories and lived experience.

But the re-presentation of these stories, here, is not without complicating presences and absences. For one, the women who told me their stories are lost to me now, relocated throughout the world through a resettlement process that continued well beyond our initial meetings. In the interim between then, when we met and knew each other, and now, when we are separated by time and distance, there are the stories that we recorded, lifted up and out of their original contexts, circulated far beyond their original owners.

The stories continue on in the grounding of ethical considerations and relationships tied to the deeply contextualized singularity of ethnographic literacy research and to listening and telling conducted in a time and place, carried forward into an uncertain and already contaminated future.

8. *HĀMĪ KHĒLCHAŬ SANGĪNĪ* / WE SING AND DANCE TOGETHER AS FRIENDS: LITERACIES ON THE MOVE AND IN SENSUOUS COALITION

Hāra-mālā, hāra-mālā rakṣā garna,
Hāmī khelchaŭ sangīnī.
To protect our way of life,
We sing and dance together as friends.
—A song and dance of women friends,
recorded in Beldangi II camp, June 2013[1]

Snapshot: Durga (United States)
Tucson, Spring 2012

A couple of evenings a week, Gopal holds a citizenship class at the mutual assistance association where he worked. This citizenship class provids a community-based alternative to other citizenship classes—run through local organizations, churches, libraries, and nonprofits—that mainly staffed classrooms with English-speaking volunteers. Gopal's class is taught in Nepali and English with significant codeswitching between the two languages. Every evening the students in attendance help Gopal carry plastic folding tables from a storage room into the classroom, neatly organizing them one after the other in front of a large whiteboard bolted to a partial wall. Chatting mostly in Nepali as they worked to set up the classroom, Gopal's students comprise of older adults: husbands, wives, and extended family members representing at least two generations of

Bhutanese refugees, meeting with the expressed goal of learning to become US citizens.

The goal of attaining citizenship in the United States is particularly important to the Bhutanese students in Gopal's citizenship class. The students I speak with tended to identify by their nationality—Bhutanese—rather than their ethnolinguistic background or caste—Tamang, Gurung, Brahman—since it was this nationality, and its subsequent removal by Bhutanese authorities, that defined them as refugees and thus eligible for resettlement. Citizenship and citizenship classes play an important role in helping those who identified as Bhutanese refugees negotiate contradictory and competing discourses around identity and social change. For example, participants often speak of the differences between their childhoods in Bhutan and the more "Americanized" lives of their children in the United States. Gopal, for one, was certain that his children would soon forget what it meant to be a Nepali-speaking Bhutanese. For him, this is because his children had grown up mostly in the refugee camps and did not remember Bhutan. Now, living out their early adult lives in the US, Gopal is sure that "they will have more American friends than they have Nepali, and they will be most of the time talking in English." At the same time, Gopal feels and teaches his students that becoming a US citizen was "one of the highest privileges" attainable, one that comes with "more responsibility" and the "hope" that "our children and some of the grandchildren . . . will know the laws of the land and will go to the schools and will be advancing." According to Gopal, it is his job as the instructor of the community-based citizenship class and a de facto social worker to help his fellow Bhutanese negotiate critical issues of citizenship, and to do so in a language they could understand through examples drawn from the uniquely Nepali-speaking Bhutanese experience of transnationalism.

Durga attends her husband's citizenship class in the evenings but had stopped going to the other ESL classes around town after she obtained work as a caregiver to an elderly Indian woman, which kept her busy most mornings of the week. In the afternoons, she would do the shopping and cooking for her family. Sometimes she babysits her grandson and teaches him the Nepali words for things around the house, but especially food—"*dyood*" (for milk), "*bhaat*" (for rice), she says, overemphasizing the vowel sounds for effect. At the time of our interviews, there are six people living in Gopal and Durga's three-bedroom apartment, including their two sons, a daughter-in-law, and their grandson. Durga's in-laws and a couple of nephews live in nearby apartments and often stopped over for tea or a bite to eat. Durga is always willing to play host to them and to her extended circle of neighbors and friends, many of whom, having heard of my research, would drop by unannounced during our interviews to listen in and add to the conversation.

My interviews with Durga often took place in her kitchen. During one such interview, Durga works adeptly at slicing mango and chopping green chili while switching in and out of English and Nepali. Our conversation begins meandering when Durga moves to the pantry and comes back with a fresh cucumber and some yellow onions. She excitedly begins explaining that these had come from the community garden located up the street from her apartment complex, at a local elementary school. She impresses upon me the difference between these vegetables and the store-bought ones she purchased at the Mexican grocery on the east side of town. Differences in size, color, texture, and taste made Durga prefer her homegrown vegetables to the grocery-store variety. They are "organic," she exclaims several times!

Durga is a member of a community garden project started by the Bhutanese Mutual Assistance Association of Tucson in collaboration with the nearby public elementary school. The project consists of fourteen recently resettled Bhutanese families, many members of whom attended Gopal's citizenship classes and participated in the kirtan mandali, cultural singing and chanting groups held at Gopal and Durga's house. In addition to growing cucumber, lettuce, onion, pumpkin, carrot, eggplant, and beans, the families engage in a tree-planting project around the school grounds.

Durga animatedly describes her role "at the garden school," tending to her family's plot at least once a week and on the weekends. She combines the vegetables from the plot with those she bought at the grocery in creating meals and snacks for all the family and guests she hosted at her apartment. Each new crop provides an occasion for remembering what life used to be like when Durga lived on the farm in Bhutan, as well as an occasion for the assessment and critique of the present, with these homegrown vegetables being better somehow than store-bought ones. Additionally, so close to the border with Mexico, it is not unusual to find Durga chopping away at a vegetable salad in her kitchen or heating oil in a fry pan in anticipation of afternoon guests while aptly considering the differences and similarities among the South Asian food items, like puri, that inspires her Nepali cooking at home, and comparable Mexican food items, like tortillas, about which she had only recently learned. She is also learning how to cultivate certain plants in the desert, which required an altogether different set of skills from the kind of cultivation she was used to in the wet, verdant jungles of southeastern Nepal and southern Bhutan. Durga, along with some other members of the community garden project, had been partnering with a science teacher at the elementary school to learn about desert irrigation systems and to set up drip irrigation for their garden plots and tree-planting project.

Snapshot: To Sing and Dance Together as Friends (Nepal)
Beldangi II camp, May 2013

Just after her last class of the day, Amashi and I walk back to the instructors' planning quarters, a bamboo hut set off from the classrooms near the entrance to the Beldangi II Spoken English Center. Sitting at a long wooden bench opposite a desk with a nameplate that reads "In-charge," we discuss Amashi's extended relationship to the language center.

Amashi is thirty years old, unmarried, and living alone in the camps as she waits on a complicated resettlement case. She has taught English in the camps for most of her twenties, serving as the in-charge at the Beldangi II Spoken English Center from the start of resettlement. These past few months, however, Amashi has taken a break from teaching to attend to her resettlement process. She has just recently returned to the center as a teacher to stay indefinitely as she waits for her case to move through the labyrinthine resettlement process.

Amashi's connection to the center is palpable. It is clear from her body language that she lives and breathes teaching. Her movements are effortless. She glides around precariously placed stacks of books as she graciously invites me into the instructors' quarters, reinforcing to me her ownership over the instructional space. As the former in-charge during the heyday of the center's activities, Amashi supervised a team of a dozen or more English teachers and led active recruiting sessions throughout her local sector, mobilizing older camp residents to come to class to learn English before departing for resettlement. She recalls the earliest days of adult education in the camp, when classes were run ad hoc and on a volunteer basis, unincentivized by donor agencies. Teachers from within the camp's English-medium secondary school system would spend their afternoons teaching classes to adult learners out of their school's broom closet. Eventually, these volunteers would organize themselves to establish what was now the Beldangi II Spoken English Center at the site of a primary school that had shut down, as families with school-age children began leaving the camps in droves for the United States and other third-country resettlement sites. The creation of the center at the location of the closed primary school was a labor of love that emerged out of the field of resettlement's exigencies.

Amashi recalls the center being, at first, "like a desert . . . so horrible!

"Then we came with the learners and the learners were so frustrated to be here and they . . . felt the center was not good.

"We got a lot of problems here. The school had been totally misused before our arrival, and it was really difficult for us to bring it to this state. Our day guards and night guards worked a lot here. They managed all the fencing, and they made the grounds and the gardens here, everything!

"Then we requested learners to bring flowers and plants, and the Lutheran World Federation gave us seedlings and we planted them here. So, we did several things to make this center this much."

Over a twenty-year displacement, the people living in the camp had found a kind of rhythm to life that was now being upended by the resettlement process. As the process unfolded, schools and domiciles were abandoned and, unattended to, invited illegal activities. Amashi describes having to fend off drug users and criminals from camping out in the school, while she worked with camp officials, a sponsoring NGO, and local community members to rebrand the abandoned school as a legitimate and recognizable location for adult learning. Eventually the center would become a space where women would come to participate in the critical solidarity it provided, as a space that supported them across cultural, language, and spiritual differences to navigate resettlement tensions and reinscribe literacy practices.

During my research, I work closely with Amashi and other teachers who helped to facilitate groups of students in coming together around a conversational topic or focus that might help illuminate center issues. One particular focus group centering on language and caste differences among women learners highlighted for me the very points Amashi was alluding to in her story of the creation of the center. Women gravitated to the center as a space of gathering. They tended to it and nurtured it like their own gardens, planting seedlings and flowers, taming the wild grasses that grew up around the classrooms. They gathered as friends, despite their differences, to serve in the creating and maintaining of a community that would support them through the resettlement process.

Sitting in a circle one afternoon inside Amashi's classroom, I spoke with nineteen women who regularly attended English class about the effects of caste and language differences on their relationships and learning at the center.

"If we cut ourselves, our blood will be the same," says a woman at the far end of the group.

"We are all friends here," others join in agreement with the woman's sentiments.

"Though we are different castes, our race is Nepali!" says another member of the group.

"Everyone's blood is the same. No one's blood is either thicker or thinner than anyone else's," says another.

"What other purposes does the center serve?" I ask, attempting to push beyond platitudes.

"If we have tension outside regarding anything, we will have no tension inside here" begins a Rai woman in her late forties.

"We are all friends here, and we gather together to enjoy."

Others chime in:

"We carry the load of tensions, but we will feel light coming here," says a nearby woman of high caste.

"We unload the load here. We feel peace. If there is something in our mind it will become cool. Tension runs away."

"I feel the same way!"

"All the problems run away."

"If we get a chance to study, we will be able to meet with friends."

"I meet with many friends here."

"I feel the same."

A month later, near the end of my research fellowship in Nepal, I sat in the Beldangi II Spoken English Center for the last time before leaving the camps. It was June 2013. The students and teachers had prepared a farewell ceremony for me that overlapped with the closing of another four-month batch of classes. To mark the occasion, classes were canceled for the day as Spoken English Center participants had prepared several hours of ceremonial tika, speeches, singing, dancing, and other performances. About midway through the ceremony, several women gathered in front of the crowd that had formed, and they began to sing and dance a sangini, a song and dance of women friends.

Hāra-mālā, hāra-mālā rakṣā garna,
Hāmī khelchaũ sangīnī.
To protect our way of life,
We sing and dance together as friends.

Isvarakō kināra mā phulai phuliyō;
Isvarāi ujyālō.

On the banks of God's pond, flowers blossomed;
divine light.

Skūla mā phulai phuliyō;
skūla ujyālō.
At the school, flowers blossomed;
the school is bright.

A sangini is a traditional song and dance performed by women during Tij, a seasonal event and celebration of friendship and marriage. But this sangini was different. Recontextualized within a spoken language and literacy program situated in the premigration context of a massive refugee resettlement process, this performance interlaced with women's investments in literacy learning tied to their resettlement. Reaching deep across the religious, ethnolinguistic, caste, and generational differences among women at the center, the effect of the performance is evocative, intimating a collective, diasporic sensing, knowing, and understanding of one another. As a literacy event, this sangini is as an expression of women's language and literacy investments being not entirely instrumental but also performative of their sensuous coalition and devotion to learning.

In the previous chapter, I explored two snapshots of women learning English on either side of the resettlement process through the lens of Susmita, Suk Maya, and Abi Maya's literacy stories. In their stories, literacy reflections lead to a reordering of experience and a reckoning with the contradictions within experience, especially women's experience of the absence of literacy education in their lives. Through intimating the tensions and contradictions of their experiences of learning later in life in their stories and conversations, women call into question the value of English and of literacy education for resettlement.

In this chapter, I explore an additional set of snapshots depicting women's moving literacies across resettlement locations as emerging from the contingencies of their migrations and yet inextricably intertwined with their efforts to form solidarity and coalitional possibilities. This time, returning to the stories of Kausila and Kali Maya, I find more evidence for women's investments in literacy as a call to coalitional ethics versus a desire to acquire functional literacy. Ultimately, this chapter argues for a revaluing of language and literacy experience in transnational literacy research beyond functional approaches. Read through the lens of Kausila and Kali Maya's literacy stories and investments, performances, like the *sangīnī* above, weave the past into the present, forming temporal, place-based connections via sensuous collaborations, embodied encounters, and women's singing and dancing together as friends.

The two snapshots in this chapter illustrate different transnational literacies on the move: Durga's knowledge of gardening and plant life brought to bear in the post-resettlement context of Tucson's language and literacy support for newcomers, and Amashi's adult English language class in the camps. These snapshots depict spaces of language, literacy, and learning on either side of the resettlement process that are used to catalyze friendship and community. These spaces are embodied, ecological, artistic, and creative, improvisational spaces where women innovate new relationships to one another through their language, literacy, and learning.

In the first snapshot, Durga's story is a story of language, learning, and love: love of family, love of land, and love of community, of cultivating belonging in relational ecologies. In the camps, Durga was an elected unit leader of the Bhutanese Refugee Women's Forum, an honorable position that would have put her in close contact with camp officials and international nongovernmental organization (INGO) workers. Though everyone spoke Nepali in the days before resettlement to English-speaking countries was an option, most women were not literate in the language. Durga was one of a few women who participated in Nepali literacy classes organized by the INGO Oxfam in the early 1990s and thus had an advantage in being even minimally able to read and write in Nepali.

Many women had been frightened out of going to the classes by angry husbands and by larger cultural attitudes that precluded married women from education. Several women I had spoken to in the refugee camps recalled hiding their schoolbooks underneath their clothes to avoid being taunted, even spit at, on their way to school. Luckily, Gopal supported Durga's literacy education as well as her work for the women's forum. Still, there was a sense in Durga's family that her education was different from Gopal's and was lacking in some way. Durga herself described the classes she took in the camp as being "classes for elderly women," and she referred to them rather demurely.

I found her description of the classes odd, given that Durga could not have been older than thirty-five at the time the classes had been offered. Yet Durga's son, Bhagat, who had been working at the family computer in the living room during one of our interviews, confirmed that the thinking in the camp at the time was that the women's literacy classes targeted mainly married women, whom most people in the camp considered too old to learn—"old grannies," he said. The class was short-lived, running just shy of a year. In it, Durga learned to read only simple words and phrases in Nepali. She took another class a few years later offered by a community development center in her sector. There, she learned a few more words and phrases in Nepali and English. She also remembered a four-month English orientation class she took in 2008 just before her resettlement where she met many friends with whom she could commiserate about the "process."

While Durga's framing of her literacy in the camp could be described as functional, there is also the intimation of new forms of literacy action tied to something other than a progress narrative. In seeking out friendships in her classes and companions with whom she might share resettlement experiences, Durga's learning is also tied to community, healing, and the possibilities of performing stories with other women.

In the second snapshot, there continue to be examples of learning as a form of solidarity. Women describe their connection to one another as a form of kinship, where they "bleed the same blood." Discursively, they work to build a solidarity that will help them to navigate, together, the tensions of resettlement through viscerally imagined ties that bind.

The *saṅgīnī* is woman-centric. The song and dance designates a space of women's knowledge production, a space of teaching and learning through movement and skill and everyday creativity and improvisation. The women of the Spoken English Centers work across discursive and material contexts of their learning and singing and dancing to create a space of alterity, an inner sanctum for their living-English work, for negotiating the moving literacies of resettlement. In this space, they define what it means to learn without fear. They determine the virtues of attaining literacy. In the time-lapse that follows, I recall conversations with both Kausila and Kali Maya that direct me to reconsider women's literacy learning through solidarity as critical epistemic and coalitional work. In this way, my recollections of women's stories help me to reconceptualize transnational literacy practices and investments through the cultural, social, and linguistic frameworks that matter to them.

Time Lapse: Learning English as a "Performance of Possibility"
I recall sitting on the damp, patchworked bedspread of Kausila's cot that is pushed back against a darkened corner of the bamboo hut where Kausila has lived for the past twenty years. I'm sitting next to Geeta, who is perched attentively at the end of bed waiting for our interview to begin. Kausila disappears behind the drawn curtain of a lopsided doorframe partitioning two rooms and returns a few moments later with a collection of tattered and molded documents and identity cards. Geeta and I handle them, gently, intrigued by the way each of the items offers a partial print of Kausila's unique migration story. Our conversation meanders for well over an hour in the middle of another sweltering day.

On the record, Kausila relates stories about carrying her son to the schoolhouse in Bhutan, how they had to climb a steep hill to get there, how she fought to send him to school when the teachers questioned his age. She speaks in hushed tones about her adult daughter's children running loose in the camps, about how her daughter's marriage to a local put the entire family's resettlement case on hold, about her hopes and fears related to these circumstances.

"The reason I study English," she says, "is when I go abroad everything will be in English.

"If we go there and ask anything in Nepali, they do not understand, but if we study English . . . well, if we come to Nepal and know Nepali is it very good. Like that, if we go abroad, we need English. That is why. Nepali doesn't work. That is why I study English.

"Another thing . . ." she says.

"I was interested to learn when I was young and now after getting a chance to study, I will go to the foreign country where English is best and needed.

"English is the main thing saying like that, by knowing or not knowing, I have learning English. That is the reason. Though I have many problems at my house, if I say I have problems at my house, I will not get time. But then also I make time and go to class.

"I feel it is important. English means wherever we go, we can speak. Nepali means only within Nepal. I feel it is useful, isn't it?"

Kausila describes the duality of her present situation at home as being full of both happiness—and grief—*sukha-dukha*. She is happy to have the opportunity to learn at this age, but she is also grieving for what has been lost in the chaos brought on by protracted migration, according to her: her eyesight, her acuity, her youth. Now that the opportunity to learn is available to her, learning is made difficult by physical ailments brought on by aging.

Kausila's narrative speaks at once to both the yearning and desiring to learn and the passage of time and the way ableist notions of adult literacy occlude what, to Kausila and others in her cohort, it means to learn, which is to be able to read English with understanding. Knowing English is not just to repeat empty words but to remember words, know them, and use them with intention.

Kausila reminds me a bit of Kali Maya, who also describes herself, in our conversations at the Spoken English Center, as very self-sufficient, better than her husband at some types of work. She says the daughter who resettled in the United States is also like this, strong. But Kali Maya is waiting to be reunited with her daughter and is in limbo because her resettlement process has been stopped by some trouble in the family, including a son who was jailed for starting a fire in the camp and two family members with special needs. Kali Maya studied in Oxfam for four months and learned to write a letter in Nepali. She remembers writing a letter to her husband while he was living out of the camp. She stopped writing, though, and slowly forgot how. She stopped attending Oxfam because of children and also feeling "What is the purpose of my study? What can *I* do?" Kali Maya has attended SEC for nearly one year, and in just four months she moved up from Grade A (preliterate) to grade B (beginner). She is known as a fast learner.

Kali Maya says that her husband did not encourage her going back to school but also didn't discourage her. He simply says nothing. She believes that women, in particular, should study and be educated in order to be courageous and self-sufficient. She says, "Our sons and grandsons will suppress us very much if we don't study! [Besides], English is needed everywhere. I have to say truly that nothing comes written in Nepali, but everything is written in English. It is very important to be able to read English."

Yet in the same way her peers express the corporeal constraints of learning later in life, Kali Maya also articulates problems remembering the letters she learns and feels discouraged that before she used to know the letters but now she is forgetting them. She says that she quickly learned to speak but is struggling with the ABCs. She wonders if she had studied regularly before her son had gone to jail whether or not she would be able to remember better. In the meantime, she complains of severe headaches and a lot of tension.

Kali Maya participates in storytelling that is a remembering, reprocessing, and reinterpreting of literacy experience in a collective context. In her story, Kali Maya forges a connection between her memories of being denied literacy education early in life and the decision she has made later in life to go to school, claiming an empowered, gendered subjecthood as an educated person who is identified with and engaged in literacy learning as oppositional struggle, to become literate "so as not to be suppressed by our sons and grandsons." This is also *sukha-dukha*, to be at once enthusiastic about the possibilities for social change tied to literacy learning and at the same time regretful of memories of denial.

＊＊＊

Kausila and Kali Maya's stories are a form of *saṅginī*, working at a theory in/of the flesh through the performance of *sukha-dukha*. Their stories enact an affective solidarity with other women through their references to lived *sukha-dukha* and to their perseverance in learning during resettlement as collective experiences and virtues. *Sukha-dukha* plays a major role in the basic categorization of Hindu theology. *Sukha* and *dukha* are most intimately connected with Hindu ideas about the nature of personhood as one comes to know oneself in relation to an ordered cosmos. *Dukha* is understood as the awareness of the limitations of experience that one must seek to transcend through spiritual education, while *sukha* is closely tied to knowledge and spiritual education through the development of a stable intellect or *gyana* (Singh et al.). Indeed, teachers at the Spoken English Center referred to their work in these terms, seeking to rid their nonliterate elders of *agyana*, or ignorance, as one of the goals of their teaching and learning.

Collectively experienced wonder and loss. Happiness and hardship. *Sukha-dukha*. While women also expressed personal desires to take advantage of resettlement imperatives and agency initiatives in order to become literate for intrinsic purposes, other collective motivations for learning seemed by far to overshadow the individual goal of learning "for myself." Learning to read and write in English was a matter, for most women, of being in relation with others, especially those they loved, to be able to write the names of their children or sign important documents on behalf of the family. In addition, women often cited meeting with friends at the language centers on a daily basis as a key motivation for learning. As Kausila put it once, "We go there in order to greet each other and share our love."

Women's stories, performances, and other artistic expressions of *sukha-dukha* frame literacy learning as a negotiation of hope and violence, of hardship and denial, as well as of joy and attainment. The *saṅginī*, a song and dance of women friends, is a particularly salient example of this negotiation. Among high-caste Hindu women during the seasonal celebrations of Tij and Tihar, the sangini is traditionally played as part of improvisational performances that tether women together across generational differences in their social obligations to family. It's a performance of the knotting of relationship across the natal and marital homes and of women-centric experiences across the life course. In the camps, women across caste, creed, and ethnolinguistic groups participated in Tij festivities, which were strongly linked to women's empowerment intiatives devised by the UNHCR and to implementing agencies to combat violence against women. Recontextualized within the Spoken English Centers, sangini performances invited large audiences of dozens, sometimes hundreds, of adult learners, family members, friends, neighbors, camp officials, and teachers to guard and protect women's learning spaces.

Like Durga's "garden school" or the *saṅginī* performed by the women of the Beldangi II Spoken English Center, Kausila and Kali Maya's living-English stories are performances of possibility. Situated in the learning context of resettlement's exigencies, their stories interrupt conventional associations between literacy learning and individual achievement or progress through migration. As a song and dance of women friends, their stories evoke kindred and community ties, solidarity, and connection more than individuation. Stories bind women together and help them to navigate the possibilities and constraints of learning during a protracted displacement. As a performance of possibility, women's living-English stories signal not only their complex and at times contradictory investments in language and literacy for resettlement, but also their dialogic participation in reshaping and recontextualizing the emotional and structural forces of displacement. Through their stories, women improvise and re-create new forms of belonging.

9. CONCLUSION: BETWEEN NOVICE AND EXPERT— LIVING ENGLISH, MOVING LITERACIES

Cinnu bhayō, bōlnu bhayō, hāsnu bhayō. Māyā sanga bhayō.
We got to know each other, to speak and laugh. It happened with love.

—Kausila

Inside the white stucco house of the Tucson International Alliance of Refugee Communities, I am finishing an English lesson. I am taking an eraser in one hand and wiping a whiteboard clean of acrid-smelling adverbial phrases, the pungent odor of red dry-erase marker still lingering at the front of the class. With the other hand, I am waving goodbye to a group of women moving toward the door. Metal folding chairs clang. The bustle of bodies gathering satchels and stray papers stirs up the warm, stagnant air. The air conditioner is not working again.

As I turn to wave goodbye, a woman approaches me with something enclosed in a small wrinkled fist etched with veins. Unfurling fingers, she reveals three gnarled pods resting in the palm of her hand. Cardamom. She motions for me to put them in my mouth to chew on. But I look at her quizzically. No, I think, better to drop them into my teaching bag for safekeeping. Three traveling artifacts. Symbolic threads, connecting the before and after of a life lived here and there.

—Adapted from field notes and journal entries,
United States 2012

I wish I had eaten those cardamom pods. Enjoyed the sharp tangy seeds as they cracked open in my mouth. I could have relished that moment with the woman, Tulasi, from my class instead of artifactualizing experience for my research.

The gift of those cardamoms. Such an illustration of my failure to grasp this other kind of connection that Tulasi was offering, a moving literacy that was not about acquisition but about learning how to navigate the singularity of a shared moment through the bridging of the past and the present.

As I reflect on those cardamom pods, I can hear the voices of the women I spoke with in Nepal, many of them cardamom farmers displaced from Bhutan. I return to their stories, now and again, sometimes in the form of the digital recording files I keep anonymously coded in the cloud. At around two minutes and thirty seconds on an MP3 file from 2013 titled "Beldangi 5," a recording of a group interview at the Spoken English Center office at Beldangi camp, Abi Maya's raspy voice exclaims emphatically:

"I didn't go to school!" As if the very question of whether or not she would be educated was ridiculous.

"Because of poverty," she says, "and, also, I was not allowed to go. We used to work the farm and guard against the monkeys!" she laughs.

Seti Maya agrees matter-of-factly.

"Monkeys would come and eat the corn and rice. We had to look after that."

The other women on the recording recall their early days in Bhutan, sowing the maize, looking after cows and goats, plucking out the cardamoms, and clearing the cardamom fields.

"There was no chance to study," says Devika.

"Besides," Nima joins in, "the school was very far, across two rivers. In the rainy season the rivers became very big and swept people away."

On the other hand, English seemed to be everything to their future.

"If we do not study English," Mangali asserts, "we will not know how to do anything, not even use a mobile phone."

"There will be phone calls from somewhere as all are gone abroad. We'll not be able to pick up the number for getting money [through the wire service]. That is why we must study."

Thinking back to that time at the midpoint of resettlement, I am reminded of the story Abi Maya told me in another group setting that same spring, about a shepherd who goes wandering into a forest and dies of starvation because he's not able to write a letter to his family back home requesting that they send rice.

"*Go Thalā bhōkalā māralā!*" she laughs.

"We are just like that hungry shepherd!"

I'm struck now, all these years later, by the interruptive force of Abi Maya's story, an interruption I was not able to hear when the story was first being relayed to me because of my complicity in another system of thinking and doing. At first, I understood Abi Maya and her peers to mean that English was necessary for their survival, that it mattered to them because of their precariousness. But later, another understanding began to emerge. These women were not helpless, passive recipients of NGOs' language and literacy programs. They were actively navigating the hope and violence of it all in their talking, laughter, and love for one another. Indeed, as many women intimate, solidarity is the affect of their learning. Something more radical than learning English and acquiring literate skills of reading and writing had taken root in the Spoken English Centers.

Gayatri Spivak writes that tracing complicity, like my complicity in teaching English and my promoting literacy skills development as a resource for migration at the expense of women's solidarity efforts, is only possible at an intermediary stage, a stage somewhere *between novice and expert*, the only stage where an ethics of nonmastery might be possible. I reflect on the way a certain kind of literate experience, and valuing of literacy, clouded my ability to listen seriously, deeply. I reflect on the significance of a persistent and effortful questioning engagement, on understanding the stakes involved in setting down in language the stories of others. I think about Tulasi from my class in Tucson and her cardamoms as another interruption, a reminder that there is more to learning and the desire for literacy than what can be contained in the empirical observations and inferences made of literacy practices alone.

As time passes and the distance between me and these conversations grows, I reflect on the local negotiation of literacy values, the absence of literacy, and how new forms of literacy collide in migration. I reflect on the collective, gendered literacy practices of women's literacy denial and the culturally inflected *sukha-dukha*, the hardship and happiness, that inform women's decisions to take up literacy later in life. I call into question that pursuit of literacy that sent me across the globe in search of events and practices that I had been trained to perceive as answers to the intercommunity questions that were haunting us back home in Tucson. Susmita's voice calls back to me:

"*To learn English language, it is like this. I did not know before. They didn't let us to study. There was no condition to read also. Even after coming here to Nepal, I didn't get a chance to study because of the children and the things at home. There was Oxfam, but I didn't get a chance to go there. Now I feel many different things, but I didn't get sense at that time. Finally, I have got the sense, now, at the time when I am going to die, to study!*"

I wonder if Susmita sometimes told me things that she thought I would want to hear as a white English teacher from the United States, stories about learning and persisting through adversity. She told this story to me. But she also told me about her life in Bhutan and her family's complicated resettlement case. She spoke about the passage of time in diaspora, about getting too old to learn things that she might have easily absorbed as a child or a young person. Her story certainly didn't fit the linear mold of a "pull yourself up by your bootstraps" narrative. Her way of speaking was tinged with irony and wryness. She would often play at the edges of non/literate subjectivity and identification. "*Oh, to learn at the time of dying!*" She exclaimed to me ironically at the end of another four-month batch of classes.

Coming back to these stories, again and again, I listen for interruption, for the limits of familiar frames I started out with, for the ways in which my sponsorship of a particular kind of literacy, rooted in literacy learning's progress narrative, prevented the opening of options. Sticking with an accumulation-of-literacy framework tied to that progress narrative would have channeled a certain kind of tellability while foreclosing others. But in meeting up with women and their stories as part of an ongoing critical dialogue weaving in and out of my own story, I came to find women's investments in literacy not to be a tool for personal advancement but a catalyst for interdependency. Literacy, as an object of desire and also as a source of this incredible suffering, became a shifting referent in a play of identifications across mutable timescapes and loci of enunciation more than a linguistic resource to help migration.

What are the lessons to be learned from five women who survived a protracted decades-long displacement, who took up learning English in their middle and later years of life during an ongoing resettlement process, whose futures are uncertain, and whose acquisition of language and literacy is not guaranteed? What tensions and contradictions at the heart of language and literacy learning later in life and in the cross-border contexts of diaspora do their discourses pry open? This final chapter operates as a conclusion of sorts, summarizing the listening to/(re)telling praxis described in the previous chapters and exploring the implications of this praxis for future research in language and literacy practices in transnational contexts. I begin by reflecting on what it means to listen back and how engaging in a listening/(re)telling praxis and returning again and again to women's living-English stories can reveal new intersections, new insights into how stories might function as performances of learning with the power to connect others across realms of possibility and constraint. I then discuss moving literacies as a reframing of language and literacy investments in border-crossing contexts of protracted displacement and refugee resettlement.

Listening to and (re)telling women's stories through writing about them has helped me to consider the ways in which the easy, transnational promises of English-language training programs mask more difficult dynamics. Storytelling through multisited narrative ethnography, through the re-presentation in research writing of intersecting stories of experience, reveals the complexity of literacy practices in the transnational contexts of women's (im)mobilities, but also raises questions about the ethics of representation and the claims being made by storyteller/listeners. Stories matter for these reasons. Working with stories, not as empirical evidence for the mobility of resources but as creative responses to literacy hope and the violence of literacy (see Branch), opens a realm of possibility. Rather than being thought of as discrete sets of skills within traveling repertoires, moving literacies become coconstructed, dialogic, performative, contingently articulated. They operate beyond the word work of written texts, inhering in the singularity and contingency of felt histories and shared moments, embodied in experiences that transform us from the inside out and the outside in—for example, chewing cardamom, sipping tea, giving and receiving tika, learning a new language; also, listening to/telling stories. They contaminate our collaborations with their sensuousness.

LISTENING BACK: LESSONS IN LIVING-ENGLISH STORIES

This book has been my attempt to relay living-English stories to US educators operating under the assumptions of a theory of accumulating literacies, as such stories attend to the lived dimensions of an uneven access to literacy education across the life course and in the context of refugee resettlement. I promised the women I spoke with in the Spoken English Centers that I would convey these stories to English-speaking educators working in English-dominant classrooms. This was a promise that would shape the form of our collaboration and the claims we made on each other. But this book has also been about re-envisioning scholarly perspectives on transnational literacy learning and its relationship to language in the lives of displaced women through the perspective of the learners themselves and their living-English stories. Living-English stories reveal the history of absence: of language, literacy, and hegemony and the way these dynamics play out in aging, sexed bodies and in gendered practices around literacy access and education. They operate as *sangini*—connecting women's stories across their individual experiences and inviting listeners into listening/(re)telling as co-performance.

Part I of the book focused on women's stories and how these stories evoked, enacted, and affected my framing of transnational literacies in motion. But contrary to the ways in which lived experience is typically represented in empirical studies of language and literacy use, I approached women's stories beyond just word work—evoking verbal as well as nonverbal literacies, felt and embodied experiences and histories. I did this not by "analyzing" the narrative structure of their stories or deriving conclusions from them, but through representations of listening/(re)telling praxis as a form of witnessing with restraint. Thus, Part I intervened in an accumulation theory of literacy in which literate resources pile up as they move across generations by proposing instead that we engage in people's stories of literacy as indexing complicated, often contradictory, investments in language, imaginal futures, and the experience of subjectivity.

Rather than provide empirical evidence for the acquisition of English language and literacy skills for economic border-crossings or personal advancement, women's living-English stories demonstrate another kind of investment. Women's stories are invested in navigating and negotiating, through dialogue with others, the vicissitudes of relationships that have shaped their access to language resources and education over the life course. Their stories explore the affective solidarities, feeling histories, and disrupted trajectories that lead people into and out of their desires to learn. In setting these stories apart from an accumulation framework, this book has been a leaning into and yielding to the knowledge work of other stories. Like proverbs with morals that curl up and out of the ruins left behind by modernity and fast capitalism, women's stories wrap around the literacy myth like the Nepalese kudzu that blanketed the forests where the Bhutanese refugee camps were located in southeastern Nepal. Stories were entangled and wild like the jungles from where they were conjured, not at all fitting into orderly domains of literate practice or the logic of linear acquisition.

In Part I, women's living-English stories are re-presented as effectual narratives, as narratives that put into effect knowledge of women's investments in English beyond accumulation. Women's stories are presented as a challenge to a certain kind of literacy hope that conflates the piling up and moving across of globally positioned language and literacy practices and resources with success, mobility, and self-interested border-crossings. More than providing a dataset for the accumulation and flow of global English resources, the living-English stories of the first half of this book do their more critical and liberatory work in attending to the relationship between gendered histories of access to education and women's uncertain futures in a protracted displacement. Between this history of access and an uncertain future, there is a realm of possibility and constraint that women negotiate in their conversations with me and with one another. In this sense, our living-English listening/storytelling is a performance of possibility in language investments that evoke, enact, and affect relationships beyond the successful accumulation of English language resources as the final outcome of their learning.

In Part II of this book, we returned to women's stories but from different angles and "loci of enunciation" in time as illustrated in and through the ethnographic narrativization of snapshots and time lapses. Through this narrativization relational nuances of language and literacy learning across sites of refugee resettlement in the United States and Nepal were explored. Chapter 7 worked at the grounded theme of "the absence of literacy," emerging from within and across snapshots and time lapses, not as a transnational reality but as a "literacy event" (Branch, "What"). A discussion of how women narrativize the absence of literacy as a "presence" in literacy learning contexts and in their conversations about their learning experiences followed, with implications for how these "literacy events" play out in learning contexts, investments, and the shaping of literate identities. In Chapter 8, "literacies on the move" are explored in the example of community gardening in the United States and women's solidarity-building through language learning in a refugee camp in Nepal. The discussion that follows zooms in on a particular performance, a song and dance of women friends called *saṅgīnī*, and the way *saṅgīnī* offers both an embodied and a conceptual link among women's experiences of learning before, during, and after resettlement.

Approaching listening to and (re)telling living-English stories through ethnographic narratives located in and across resettlement phases and locations, this book has proposed a way of listening to and retelling women's stories of learning as something more than representation. Rather, living-English stories invite us into dialogue and reflection with others. When we locate these narratives in cross-border processes and cross-boundary discourses in which we participate, we can recognize the urgency of considering our own lives within others' narratives. Narratives become points of departure for us to pursue further understanding of the historically specific relations between speakers and listeners and our obligations to one another, rather than representations for which the researcher claims some responsibility for a distant other.

Women's stories of language and literacy experience are not just a record of their literacy practices. As such, these stories must not be reduced to either transparent renderings of transnational realities or as empirical evidence of "literacy." Rather, living-English stories might be engaged critically as a form of dialogical knowledge-making and a response to the tensions and contradictions of learning English in a protracted displacement and during an ongoing resettlement process. These stories might help us rethink transnational literacy learning beyond accumulation, as a process of navigating and negotiating external forces. Rethinking transnational literacy as living-English stories gives us insights into the possibilities and constraints of specific women's agency in their later-in-life learning relative to their histories and current experiences of living in diaspora.

This book has explored how women, through their literacy learning, channel the chronic chaos and uncertainty of prolonged and indefinite periods of protracted waiting into opportunities for community resilience and creative praxis. It has linked the stories of Nepali-speaking Bhutanese women across the resettlement divide, gesturing toward the ways these living-English stories not only index productive entanglements but also operate rhetorically, not merely signifying difference but intentionally crafting relational intersections for rethinking literacy hope/happiness and violence/hardship in transnational migration.

MĀYĀ SANGA BHAYŌ / "IT HAPPENED WITH LOVE": LEARNING TO LEARN FROM MOVING LITERACIES

Another argument of this book has been that while living-English stories work to reframe a theory of accumulating literacies, they are, at the same time, composed of moving literacies. By moving literacies, I mean not only linguistic repertoires, sets of language and literacy skills deployed in meaningful and persuasive communication, but also women's capacity for literate performances that move interlocutors to reconfigure and reformulate how they understand the effects of literacy hope and violence in a precarious world. Moving literacies does not refer to English-only reading and writing literacies, and neither does it refer to literacy development within plurilingual repertoires. Instead, moving literacies are sets of navigational skills and capacities for working through the tensions and contradictions of social change and resettlement. Moving literacies are more than word work; they involve everyday creativity beyond the linguistic, including the semiotic, embodied, and performative. Moving literacies challenge the notion of linear language and literacy development by including all of the emergent and uneven and dialogic knowledge work around and through which literacy practices are taken up or not.

The moving literacies of this book are a dialogic performance of the possibilities and constraints of learning English, a lively assemblage of enunciations and negotiations, situated in the context of an ongoing protracted displacement and refugee resettlement process. This book brings the local, the embodied, and the mutable to bear on questions of literacy and mobility within the field of rhetoric and writing studies to rethink literacy as both a cultural practice and a means of creating and maintaining translocal ties.

In our narrative encounters, women use their moving literacies to point to and help us navigate interdependency within complex relational ties that emerge, shift, and evolve throughout a protracted displacement. In one such meeting, Kausila describes the advantages to coming together at the Spoken English Centers to learn. She says, *Cinnu bhayō, bōlnu bhayō, hāsnu bhayō. Māyā sanga bhayō.* "We met, spoke, and laughed. It happened with love." This is "loving perception" (Lugones), a listening/speaking praxis that goes beyond agonism, or channeled conflict, in its seeking to yield to the affectionate recognition of an-other across differences. Indeed, throughout the book, we encounter conversations, dialogues, stories, and performances in which women engage creatively and playfully within the tricky dynamism of the dislocation and relocation of family members, friends, and neighbors, while their own resettlement cases hang precariously before them. Kausila's invocation of *sukha-dukha*, for example, in women's coming together to learn later in life and for a resettlement they did not want, nor could have imagined previously, is a moving literacy that binds them together in loving perception of one another's experience.

Women narrate their individual experiences of learning English in images, idioms, stories, and performances that recontextualize personal struggles in collective history and contribute to a community consciousness and solidarity. By reframing transnational literacy learning through living-English stories composed of moving literacies, this book has engaged in a listening/telling praxis that defies the aims of the acquisition and accumulation of language and literacy resources marked by scarcity and precarity. Living-English stories shift the focus, instead, to holding space for lovingly perceiving the possibilities and constraints of our interdependency across differences in language, culture, and investments in learning. For this listening/telling praxis, there can be no omniscient, ethnographic authority, no expert in the room or on the page. It is in that space between novice and expert, at that intermediate stage, that we can set to work in learning to learn from one another.

EPILOGUE: STORIES AS *SANGĪNĪ*

I RETURN TO THE CAMPS IN THE SUMMER of 2016 to conduct follow-up interviews with teachers and learners from the language centers, but nearly everyone was gone. I find only two teachers still in the camps, and they were waiting for their resettlement dates to be announced at any time. The language centers had all closed, and nearly all of the learners had been resettled, though some, no doubt, had made plans to resettle themselves internally, blending into hillside villages in Ilam, reconnecting with family in India, slipping unnoticed into the daily rhythms of life in surrounding villages, towns, and cities. Kausila, who had been a learner at the Beldangi I language center, is nowhere to be found, gone—I hope, to Australia to live with her daughter. Susmita, Suk Maya, Kali Maya, Abi Maya, all gone. At this time, efforts are underway on the part of NGOs and local governments to close down the camps. Huts are dismantled almost as soon as families leave for resettlement. Vegetation is starting to sprout up in the ruins left behind. The jungle is closing in on what was once a thriving marketplace, a lively canteen, a secondary school. There are only traces of history left, which is the way closely managed diasporas are intended, to fall back into nonexistence, nonplace, nonhistory.

Coming back to the camps at the end of the Bhutanese resettlement process, I feel the disturbing silence of the deconstructed architecture of a protracted displacement: huts, schools, and infrastructure turned to jungle. Only the whisper of a trace left. Standing in the jungle path leading to one of the language centers, I close my eyes and recall a scene of learning, a group of women gather in a circle, cross-legged, sitting on thickly woven jute mats. Facilitated by their teacher, their focus is centered on the question of why many women in the camps were not coming to the Spoken English Centers and not interested in learning English for resettlement. At the midpoint of the resettlement process, attendance is waning at the centers. Participants are afraid the centers might close or that the UNHCR would stop supporting incentives for teaching. Suk Maya and Susmita joke heartily with each other, imagining what the women who don't attend school must be thinking.

"Elephants don't get big by reading!" Suk Maya laughs, prompting agreement from the other women.

Susmita chimes in, "Why should the people whose teeth have ripened go to school?"

Other participants agree with this vernacular way of knowing and experiencing the resettlement imperative to learn English. To the women who invest their time in learning, it is *agyān*, an ignorance that is pervasive in the camps and has deep roots in how people in the camps have experienced the absence or interruption of literacy education.

Remembering these encounters, I feel the proverbial absence of literacy to be like a ruin, on the site of which women's stories of happiness and suffering emerge to index the complex layering of meaning attached to learning English, or any language, in and through the migration process. The meanings of English twine about the exigencies of resettlement like ivy curling up and out of crumbling foundations, or like the vines that thread through the forest, encircling the Spoken English Centers.

Yet in the absence of one kind of literacy is the presence of other literacies, moving literacies, stories, like a song and dance of women friends, connecting individuals' experiences of past and present across their collective dislocations and relocations.

A large, knotted custard apple drops from the forest canopy and splits open, oozing creamy liquid. I startle back into the present moment.

The forest pulsates with living stories.

Listening to/retelling stories. *Speaking with* and *speaking to* is a moving literacy, reverberating, un/finished. Here:

We came to know of each other—
We spoke and laughed. It happened with *love*.

A BRIEF ESSAY ON METHODS

THE STORIES IN THIS BOOK ARE BASED on interviews, focus groups, participant observation, and informal conversations with women learners on either side of the Bhutanese refugee resettlement process. All the narrative encounters described in Part I took place in refugee camps in Nepal in either women's homes or in the language centers (Spoken English Centers) where women attended class daily. Classes ran five days a week for six hours a day in four-month "batches." Three levels of students made up the A, B, and C classrooms, representing "levels" of proficiency from "nonliterate" to "intermediate," as determined by local facilitators and teaching staff. I interviewed adult learners at all levels. Interviews were primarily conducted in Nepali and then transcribed in Romanized Nepali script and translated into English by me in collaboration with paid local translators from the camps and former students, as well as native Nepali speakers from outside of the camps.

I drew from the following ethnographic source materials to construct the narratives of the chapters in parts I and II: (1) transcripts from semistructured interviews with adult learners evoking literacy narratives, educational histories, and everyday practice, (2) photographic documentation of literacy artifacts in the Spoken English Centers, homes, and camp-based community spaces of many interviewees living in Nepal, and in the literacy programs, language classes, and apartment complexes of recently resettled refugees in Tucson, (3) audiovisual recordings of class observations, interviews with teachers, and field notes with regard to specific lessons, activities, and in-class literacy work, and (4) transcripts of semiformal participant focus groups conducted at the Spoken English Centers in Nepal and facilitated by local instructors.

In total, while conducting research in the United States, I observed about a dozen classes, interviewed sixteen adult learners, ten teachers, two program staff members, and four coordinators/executive staff members. While in Nepal, I conducted three sets of thirty-five individual interviews, several group interviews, fourteen teacher interviews, and ten focus groups totaling approximately one hundred participants. Informal interviews with Spoken English Center participants and staff also played a role in the ongoing research, serving as follow-up to themes generated in more structured interviews or observed during focus groups' sessions. These informal interviews included countless conversations before and after classes and sometimes during classroom activities after I was invited by teachers and participants to comment on lessons or document literacy work in action. By contrast, the semistructured interviews drew from more formalized models of qualitative interview methodology, including Irving Seidman's three-part interview structure for education-related interviewing and Norma González, Luis Moll, and Cathy Amanti's funds of knowledge interview scheme, also a three-part series of interviews structured around participants' perspectives on everyday life and schooling and its relationship to larger social and economic influences.

In most instances, I was able to meet with and record individual interviewees on three different occasions. The first meeting involved an informal survey of biographical information and migration history. In the second meeting, I asked participants to describe a typical day in the camp, and we discussed different aspects of family life and obligation. During the third meeting, we spoke more specifically about learning English, future goals, and the resettlement process. Interview questions were in general open-ended, flexible, and varied according to the individual. Each interview lasted anywhere from twenty minutes to over an hour and sometimes involved house visits and more informal chatting over tea or lunch, although most interviews began at the Spoken English Centers and were conducted before, after, or in lieu of class.

For interviews conducted during the earlier months of research in Nepal, I asked Spoken English Center instructors to help facilitate the process. In most cases, this meant that I would attend Spoken English Center teacher meetings and planning sessions, facilitate needs assessments, and meet with the center in-charge before an interview to generate, review, revise, and/or rehearse a set of questions. I sought guidance from specific instructors in selecting participants for the individual interviews through a mixed process of first snowball and then theoretical sampling (choosing participants based on how well they might be able to contribute to the developing theory related to the project). As the in-charge was often free from teaching duties in the late morning and early afternoon, I enlisted them to assist with the interview, to ask questions, and to translate language that was unfamiliar to me.

My reasons for enlisting the in-charge were as follows: (1) The in-charge and instructors at the center expressed interest in and desire to help with the research; (2) The in-charge was from the same community as the participants (in fact, instructors, in-charges, and learners often lived next door to one another, and the nature of informal education in the Spoken English Center was one of mutual respect and community-based learning since the learners trusted and respected their teachers); (3) The in-charge was familiar with the different ways of speaking Nepali, especially among older learners, and would easily be able to translate cultural allusions and metaphors that were not obvious to me at the time of research; and (4) subsequently, with this insider knowledge, the in-charge could modify the interview scheme to follow the flow and direction of the interview as per the learner's narrative. However, as my knowledge of Nepali grew, I was able to conduct many of the later interviews on my own with little facilitation by the in-charge. I worked with a former Spoken English Center instructor and trained researcher from the camp to translate and transcribe the interviews from the original Nepali into English, a process that took approximately three months and involved over a hundred separate transcriptions. The other sources of data, including the classroom observations, documentation of literacy work, and teacher interviews, were noted and transcribed by me. The transcriptions were used to compare and contrast themes that emerged overall.

Upon returning to the United States and to my adult literacy classes in Tucson, I began conducting follow-up interviews with former students and their families, tracing their continued movements across the US and triangulating observations and field notes from my stay in the refugee camp. I continued the analysis of data already started in Nepal, using the grounded theory methods described by Kathy Charmaz and Linda Liska Belgrave in "Qualitative Interviewing and Grounded Theory Analysis." Charmaz and Belgrave's grounded approach to analysis consists of series of guidelines that attempt to aid researchers in developing theory from qualitative data collection and analysis. The first step is to identify recurring themes in the data via open and focused coding of interview and focus-group transcripts and field notes. I applied the method as follows. After establishing some general themes, I returned to the data to determine more focused codes and generate taxonomies. For example, after establishing "age; concepts of aging and learning" as a focused code, I went back to the data to map instances of students and teachers' talk around the topic of age and learning. I mapped instances of talk about age and learning onto different functions to see how the talk operated within a research site (the Spoken English Center) and across sites (in refugee homes in the United States) and then compared those functions with the available research/theory in the field.

It is worth mentioning here details related to informed consent and the disclosure of the research. Women were informed about and agreed to the sharing of their stories through an IRB-approved and monitored process of oral disclosure specifically designed for nonliterate participants. At each of the language centers, oral disclosure in Nepali was achieved through research collaborators (e.g., teachers, NGO-sponsored facilitators, camp residents, and UNHCR-trained translators), who explained the research to participants and helped to identify volunteers to speak with me and have their stories recorded. In addition, English-language disclosure forms were distributed to facilitators and teaching staff and kept on site at the Spoken English Centers in Nepal and at the regional suboffice of the Bhutanese Refugee Education Programme in Damak.

My agreements with the women I spoke with for this book also evolved over the course of my year-long work in the camps. At first, we entered into our storytelling contract with one another cautiously and tentatively, weighing the seen and unseen risks and benefits. Over time, some women sought me out through their teachers and friends, wanting to tell their stories to an English-speaking audience and wanting to share the details of their lives in displacement, including identifying information such as their names, camp sectors, and other personal details. However, out of an abundance of caution and concern for the privacy and confidentiality of participants, and in keeping with IRB protocols, I use pseudonyms for all the women in this book. I also conceal the locations of interviews and the specific language centers where women attended classes. While I maintain the accuracy of individuals' idiomatic forms of expression as well as identification with specific Indigenous and ethnolinguistic communities, in some cases I have transposed bits of common language and dialogue, especially around shared themes, from one women's interviews and dialogues onto others. Drawing on methods of composite narration and performance ethnography, I work at the cusp of literal translation and storytelling.

In this book, women tell their stories to me in Nepali, and I listen and (re)tell the stories here in English as part of the claims and agreements we made in relation to the stories. My original agreement with participants was that I would record their stories in Nepali and then translate them into English to make them accessible to US-based, English-speaking educators on the other side of the resettlement process. The Romanic transcription system I use in the book is adapted from systems of transcription generally accepted in Nepal, especially Chandra Rana's *Nepālī Bhāshā: Comprehensive Nepali: Speaking and Writing*, with additional support from Ralph Lilley Turner and Dorothy Rivers Turner's *A Comparative and Etymological Dictionary of the Nepali Language*,

Neural Machine Translation, and Generative AI. I also worked closely with both trained and untrained transcribers and translators inside and outside of the camps, all of whom I mention by name in the acknowledgments. Decisions about where and when to include Romanic transcriptions alongside English-language translations reflect plurilingual decision-making processes among collaborators: translators, interpreters, teachers, learners, friends, community members, and former students. Still, these decisions, while informed by my collaborations with others, have mainly rested with me, and I alone am responsible for the ways in which using a Romanic transcription system and rendering these stories in English for English-language educators and researchers falls short of the promises and possibilities of a more plurilingual approach.

NOTES

Acknowledgments

1. *The contents of this book are solely the responsibility of the author and do not necessarily represent the official views of the Fulbright Program, the Government of the United States, or the Commission for Educational Exchange between the United States and Nepal.*

Introduction. Starting Places: Language and Literacy Learning between Pre- and Post-Resettlement Contexts

1. In "No Secrets: Rigoberta's Guarded Truth," critic Doris Sommer writes, "Her testimonial is an invitation to a tête-à-tête, not to a heart to heart" (58). The tête-à-tête suggests "deferential distance" among interlocutors. "[M]aybe we are not so much outsiders as marginals," writes Sommer, "allies in a possible coalition rather than members" (59).
2. See Amy Shuman's *Other People's Stories: Entitlement Claims and the Critique of Empathy* for interesting arguments about who is entitled to stories that circulate beyond their original locations.
3. In addition to Spivak and Alcoff, I'm deeply indebted to performance-oriented, critical ethnographers' work on critical reflexivity, including Bryan Keith Alexander's notion of "making tracks" and Tami Spry's and Della Pollock's separate work on the performative "I." Alexander writes about critical reflexive writing as "a method [that] is both a demonstration and a call for a greater sense of implicating and complicating how we are always and already complicit in the scholarly productions of our labor, and the effects of our positions and positionalities within diverse communities in which we circulate . . . . Critical reflexivity becomes especially important when we cross cultural borders; when we enter other realms of experience that call us to attend to the tracks that led us to the particular place, where our presence tracks over, and what we track into other people's sacred territories" (qtd. in Madison 198).

Spry offers a research positionality committed to critical reflexivity via a concept of the "performative-I" as co-presence that shifts the orientation of the research from observation to a participation that engages with/in (1) textual forms as effects of the fragments of experience, (2) an empathetic epistemology of critical and co-present reflection with others in transforming systems of dominance, and (3) performative writing that constructs a moveable self via performative participatory engagement with others (qtd. in Madison 199). Pollock describes a performative "I" that "has a politics and an ethics" and that "[performs] displacement by error, intimacy, others [and] moves beyond the atomization, alienation, and reproduction of the authorial self toward new points of identification and alliance" (252). Pollock imagines "a mobile, performative 'I'" (247) that, quoting critical feminist theorist Mary Russo's 1994 work *The Female Grotesque: Risk, Excess and Modernity*, may even produce "new political aggregates—provisional, uncomfortable, even conflictual coalitions of bodies" (247).

4. In an interview with Nancy N. Chen, Trinh T. Minh-ha describes "speaking nearby" as "a speaking that does not objectify, does not point to an object as if it is distant from the speaking subject or absent from the speaking place. A speaking that reflects on itself and can come very close to a subject without, however, seizing or claiming it" (87). Trinh likens this speaking to poetic language that lends itself to "forms of indirectness" as well as a speaking that is "not just a technique or statement to be made verbally" but an "attitude in life, a way of positioning oneself in relation to the world" (87).

Part I. Speaking with/to: Living-English Stories

1. *An-other* is a reference to Walter Mignolo's de-linking work heavily cited in the introduction to Romeo García and Damián Baca's *Rhetorics Elsewhere and Otherwise: Contested Modernities, Decolonial Visions*: García and Baca write, "Mignolo argues, then, for geo- and body-politics of knowledge and understanding from *an-other* historical location that breaks up the illusion that 'all knowledges are and have to originate in the imperial form of consciousness' (462)" ("Introduction" 22). I use the term here to suggest a "world of learning" outside of the linear-axes model of accumulating literacies.

1. *Siknē Icchā* / "The Desire to Learn": Susmita

1. *Muuk bhaat* literally translates as "mouth rice"; a local translator working in the camps with me described this as a colloquial and

intentionally crude form of speech, a vernacular way of talking that could be translated as "rice hole"; a second translator whom I worked with many years later, without ties to the camps, suggested that the phrase should be longer: *Bhaat mukh ma halnu*—put rice in your mouth.
2. "In the village, the army used to come, and fearing that we left" is a reference to Bhutanese government occupation of villages of Nepali-speaking communities in Bhutan's southernmost districts following political unrest in the early 1990s.
3. "Sometime before, I went there to meet them" refers to illegally crossing the border to visit family during protracted displacement in Nepal.
4. "Power cut" refers to the government rationing of electricity.
5. *Drukpas*, a derogatory term for Bhutanese officials; also refers to a sect of Tibetan Buddhism.
6. "Only after 65 years, people get benefits" refers to Social Security.

2. *Ma Aphnaī lāgi Sikchu* / "I Learn for Myself!": Suk Maya

1. Suk Maya is referring to the first class in a series of three classes classified by "grade" offered at the Spoken English Centers: Grades A, B, and C. Grade A was typically composed of women learners from the camp with little or no formal school experience, who were not able to read or write in any language. Typically, Grade A students learned the English alphabet, copied letters, and memorized simple dialogues.
2. *Lotta* refers to drinking vessels.
3. *Tola* is a Nepali unit of measurement.
4. IOM refers to the International Office of Migration, the organization in charge of processing approved cases for resettlement.
5. Siliguri is a city in West Bengal on the other side of the Nepal-India border.

3. *(Malaaī) Ali-Ali (Angrējī) Āuchha* / "Just a Little (English) Comes (to Me)": Kali Maya

1. "There" refers to abroad, or a third-country resettlement location.
2. "Same district but different block" refers to Sarpang District in the south of Bhutan; the family shifted places within the district from Gelephu to Danabari. Note: Place names have been altered to protect confidentiality.
3. "[U]nder the sisoo trees" was a common phrase used by older adults in the camp when recalling educational efforts in the early days of

the camps. Before there were sponsoring and implementing agencies, Bhutanese refugees organized educational activities ad hoc and with little resources "on the grounds and in the jungles under the sisoo trees."
4. Kali Maya is most likely referring to the 1988 census in Bhutan, in which the Bhutanese government aimed to "'identify foreigners and issue citizenship identity cards to all bonafide Bhutanese nationals'" (Royal Government of Bhutan, qtd. in Hutt 152). As part of the census, individuals were added to a list marked F1 to F7, delineating various degrees of relationship to the state from "F1 Genuine Bhutanese citizens" to "F7 Non-nationals, i.e., migrants and illegal settlers" (*Bhutan: Human Rights Violations*; also qtd. in Hutt 154). Kali Maya's husband was identified as F1 Genuine Bhutanese Citizen.
5. "[M]edical is already done" refers to a point in the resettlement process when individuals must undergo a medical examination. This examination usually comes close to the end of the process just before an individual or family receives their date to be resettled.
6. "[F]or cheating at the time of our interview" refers to what Kali Maya suspects is the cause of her resettlement process suspension, that the family was found to be fraudulent during the medical interview when they did not disclose the son's drug use.
7. "[A]ge . . . not suitable for marriage" refers to the marriage/elopement of minors, often without parents' permission.
8. "Vulnerable status" refers to the Unaccompanied Refugee Minors program in the United States.
9. "Fathers" refers to Jesuit priests from India posted to the CARITAS Nepal's Bhutanese Refugee Education Programme as field officers by the sponsoring agency Jesuit Refugee Service, Delhi.

4. *Go Thala Bhōkalā Mārala* / "The Hungry Shepherd Died":
Abi Maya

1. *Fapar* refers to a bitter grain.
2. Number 7 refers to the 1988 census system of classification of Bhutanese citizens; see Chapter 3, footnote 4 above.
3. "They used to say, 'something, something,' . . . ." Here, Abi Maya is describing the confusion and rumors in her village following the census. It was not clear to Abi Maya or her friends, neighbors, and family at the time what was meant by the census, and there was general fear and suspicion of government officials. Information flowed

from various channels, and it was not clear what was accurate information and what was rumor.
4. "Many people fled, but *we* were taken out for being in the number 7 category," meaning that people in Abi Maya's village left for many different reasons, but her family left because they were grouped by the 1988 census into the category of "non-nationals, i.e., migrants and illegal settlers."
5. "From time to time, *they* used to come asking, 'Your date for leaving is now, when will you leave?'" refers to governmental officials.
6. "After that we came and stayed in India, but because some of my relatives were in Nepal, we were taken here and placed as refugees." It is not clear from the dialogue who took Abi Maya and her family to Nepal.
7. *Jethi mathi* means "sister above"; in this context, a euphemism for first wife.
8. Like many of the Nepali-speaking people displaced from Bhutan, Abi Maya and her family were uncertain about where to go or stay after crossing the border into India. Those without family or permanent connections in India eventually made their way to Nepal (see Hutt, *Unbecoming Citizens*, for a deeper explanation about how this was orchestrated).

5. *Gharkō Sukha-Dukha Jastai Hō* / "(Learning English) Is Just Like the Joys and Sorrows of Home": Kausila

1. Women often spoke about the difficulty of accessing rural schools from their farming villages. Floods and landslides often prevented families from sending their children to school.
2. *Mātrā* are Nepali vowel symbols.
3. Kausila is describing an experience common among women who attended the Oxfam Nepali literacy classes. There was community backlash against NGO efforts to educate women, and the women who attended the Oxfam classes were often harassed and assaulted on their way to school, while also being mocked and made the subject of gossip. Women describe being spit on, having their books destroyed, and having rocks thrown at them on the way to school. A decade later, with resettlement on the horizon, attitudes became more tolerant of and less severe toward adult education, though resistance to women's education, especially among older women, continued to quietly persist throughout the resettlement process.
4. In this passage, Kausila continues to describe her work in the Oxfam classes, and how she "studied Nepali nicely," etc. It is not

clear from the background she provides to what extent she could read or write before Oxfam arrived. The story of the Oxfam representative that Kausila relays suggests that others may have assumed her to be highly literate, though Kausila claims she was not educated in Bhutan.
5. Kausila is suggesting that her husband may have left her because of disagreements they had about her education.
6. Kausila is referring to Australia, where one of her daughters is resettled and where Kausila is currently applying to go.
7. Kausila describes her conflicting feelings about resettlement. There is a sense here that, just as she describes her feelings of terror, she does not want to appear too negative about the future. She moves between happiness and sorrow.

6. Storyteller Learning and Doing / "Listening Back": Katie

1. The title of this chapter is a reference to Shirley Brice Heath's ethnographer positionality—the ethnographer learning and doing—in *Ways with Words: Language, Life, and Work in Communities and Classrooms.*

Part II. Learning to Learn: Situating Stories across Languages, Locations, and Time

8. *Hāmī Khēlchaū Sangīnī* / "We Sing and Dance Together as Friends": Literacies on the Move and in Sensuous Coalition

1. The translation of these song lyrics has perplexed me for over a decade. They come from an impromptu *sangīnī*, a song and dance of women friends, that the women of the Beldangi II Spoken English Center performed at my leaving ceremony during my last weeks in the camp. I recorded the dance and played it for a friend of mine from the camps who had resettled and was living in Tucson when I returned to the United States from Nepal. She transcribed the first line of song's refrain as "haramala haramala raksha gara" and translated it as "protect us and our way of life." But when I went to cross-reference the translation of *haramala* in Turner and Turner's *Comparative and Etymological Dictionary of the Nepali Language,* I could not find a match. Google Translate did not help either! Several years later, in a second round of translation work with a friend of a colleague who was not from the camps, the trouble continued. The second translator could find no equivalent for *haramala* and was convinced that the word should be *hāmrō* (our). I even changed

the lyrics based on this suggestion for an article I was writing at the time, while keeping the first translator's meaning intact—"protect our way of life." Later, I would come to believe that *haramala* is not one word but two: *hāra-mālā,* meaning garland or rosary in Hindi (*hāra*) and Nepali (*mālā*). The garland represents women's way of life in the camps, just as the first translator had suggested. Its meaning is interconnected and circular, tied to the seasons and to divinity. The lyrics that follow the refrain bear this out. They are about flowers that blossom on the banks of God's pond and in the school and describe women taking the flowers and decorating themselves with them in a blessing. Today, I can't say for sure whether the women I recorded so long ago in the camps were singing about *hāra-mālā* or if *hāra-mālā* is a mistranslation, but I can say what "not knowing" represents: the knotty work of translation, of engaging in listening and telling in the space between novice and expert; of the exquisitely tedious and humbling work of "learning to learn" that Spivak writes about in the "Afterword" of her translation of Mahasweta Devi's stories, of an ongoing commitment to being in-process.

WORKS CITED AND CONSULTED

Abu-Lughod, Lila. *Veiled Sentiments: Honor and Poetry in a Bedouin Society*. U of California P, 1986.

———. "Writing against Culture." *Recapturing Anthropology: Working in the Present*, edited by Richard G. Fox, School of American Research Press, 1991, pp. 137–62.

Ahearn, Laura M. *Invitations to Love: Literacy, Love Letters, and Social Change in Nepal*. U of Michigan P, 2001.

Alcoff, Linda. "The Problem of Speaking for Others." *Cultural Critique*, no. 20, 1991, pp. 5–32.

Behar, Ruth. *Translated Woman: Crossing the Border with Esperanza's Story*. Beacon Press, 1993.

———. *The Vulnerable Observer: Anthropology That Breaks Your Heart*. Beacon Press, 1996.

Bhutan: Human Rights Violations against the Nepali-Speaking Population in the South. Amnesty International, 1992.

Bowen, Lauren Marshall. "Composing a Further Life: Introduction to the Special Issue." *Literacy in Composition Studies*, vol. 6, no. 2, 2018, pp. vi–xxvi.

Branch, Kirk. "Literacy Hope and the Violence of Literacy: A Bind That Ties Us." Review of *Collaborative Imagination: Earning Activism through Literacy Education*, by Paul Feigenbaum; *The Lure of Literacy: A Critical Reception of the Compulsory Composition Debate*, by Michael Harker; *Transiciones: Pathways of Latinas and Latinos Writing in High School and College*, by Todd Ruecker; and *Producing Good Citizens: Literacy Training in Anxious Times*, by Amy Wan, *College English*, vol. 79, vol. 4, 2017, pp. 407–20.

———. "What No Literacy Means: Literacy Events in the Absence of Literacy." *Reflections*, vol. 9, no. 3, 2010, pp. 52–74.

Brandt, Deborah. "Accumulating Literacy: Writing and Learning to Write in the Twentieth Century." *College English*, vol. 57, no. 6, 1995, pp. 649–68.

———. *Literacy in American Lives.* Cambridge UP, 2001.

———. "Sponsors of Literacy." *College Composition and Communication*, vol. 49, no. 2, 1998, pp. 165–85.

Brandt, Deborah, and Katie Clinton. "Limits of the Local: Expanding Perspectives on Literacy as a Social Practice." *Journal of Literacy Research*, vol. 34, no. 3, 2002, pp. 337–56.

Brown, Timothy. "Improving Quality and Attainment in Refugee Schools: The Case of the Bhutanese Refugees in Nepal." *Learning for a Future: Refugee Education in Developing Countries*, edited by Jeff Crisp et al., UNHCR, 2001, pp. 109–61.

Calafell, Bernadette M. "Rhetorics of Possibility: Challenging the Textual Bias of Rhetoric through the Theory of the Flesh." *Rhetorica in Motion: Feminist Rhetorical Methods and Methodologies*, edited by Eileen E. Schell and K. J. Rawson, U of Pittsburgh P, 2010, pp. 104–17.

Charmaz, Kathy, and Linda Liska Belgrave. "Qualitative Interviewing and Grounded Theory Analysis." *The SAGE Handbook of Interview Research: The Complexity of the Craft*, edited by Jaber F. Gubrium et al., SAGE Publications, 2012, pp. 347–66.

Chen, Nancy N. "'Speaking Nearby': A Conversation with Trinh T. Minh-ha." *Visual Anthropology Review*, vol. 8, no. 1, 1992, pp. 82–91.

Craig, Sienna R. *The Ends of Kinship: Connecting Himalayan Lives between Nepal and New York.* U of Washington P, 2020.

———. "Migration, Social Change, Health, and the Realm of the Possible: Women's Stories between Nepal and New York." *Anthropology and Humanism*, vol. 36, no. 2, 2011, pp. 193–214.

Cushman, Ellen, et al. "Delinking: Toward Pluriversal Rhetorics." *College English*, vol. 84, no. 1, 2021, pp. 7–32.

Davis, Coralynn V. *Maithil Women's Tales: Storytelling on the Nepal-India Border.* U of Illinois P, 2014.

Duffy, John M. "Never Hold a Pencil: Rhetoric and Relations in the Concept of 'Preliteracy.'" *Written Communication*, vol. 17, no. 2, 2000, pp. 224–57.

———. "Other Gods and Countries: The Rhetorics of Literacy." *Towards a Rhetoric of Everyday Life: New Directions in Research on Writing, Text, and Discourse*, edited by Martin Nystrand and John Duffy, U of Wisconsin P, 2003, pp. 38–57.

———. *Writing from These Roots: Literacy in a Hmong-American Community.* U of Hawaii P, 2007.

García, Romeo. "Creating Presence from Absence and Sound from Silence." *Community Literacy Journal*, vol. 13, no. 1, 2019, pp. 7–15.

Ghabra, Haneen Shafeeq, and Bernadette Marie Calafell. "Intersectional Reflexivity and Decolonial Rhetorics: From Palestine to Aztlán." *Rhetorics Elsewhere and Otherwise: Contested Modernities, Decolonial Visions*, edited by Romeo García and Damián Baca. CCCC/NCTE, 2019, pp. 62–84.

González, Norma, Luis C. Moll, and Cathy Amanti, editors. *Funds of Knowledge: Theorizing Practices in Households, Communities, and Classrooms*. Lawrence Erlbaum Associates, 2005.

Graff, Harvey J. *The Legacies of Literacy: Continuities and Contradictions in Western Culture and Society*. Indiana UP, 1987.

———. *The Literacy Myth: Literacy and Social Structure in the Nineteenth-Century City*. Academic Press, 1979.

Heath, Shirley Brice. *Ways with Words: Language, Life, and Work in Communities and Classrooms*. Cambridge UP, 1983.

Hutt, Michael. *Unbecoming Citizens: Culture, Nationhood, and the Flight of Refugees from Bhutan*. Oxford UP, 2003.

Jackson, Rachel C., and Dorothy Whitehorse DeLaune. "Decolonizing Community Writing with Community Listening: Story, Transrhetorical Resistance, and Indigenous Cultural Literacy Activism." *Community Literacy Journal*, vol. 13, no. 1, 2019, pp. 37–54.

Kynard, Carmen. "This Bridge: The BlackFeministCompositionist's Guide to the Colonial and Imperial Violence of Schooling Today." *Feminist Teacher*, vol. 26, nos. 2–3, 2016, pp. 126–41.

Lagman, Eileen. "Moving Labor: Transnational Migrant Workers and Affective Literacies of Care." *Literacy in Composition Studies*, vol. 3, no. 3, 2015, pp. 1–24.

Lam, Wan Shun Eva, et al. "Transnationalism and Literacy: Investigating the Mobility of People, Languages, Texts, and Practices in Contexts of Migration." *Reading Research Quarterly*, vol. 47, no. 2, 2012, pp. 191–215.

Lamsal, Tika R. *Globalizing Literacies and Identities: Translingual and Transcultural Literacy Practices of Bhutanese Refugees in the US*. 2014. U of Louisville, PhD dissertation.

Lather, Patti. "Postbook: Working the Ruins of Feminist Ethnography." *Signs*, vol. 27, no. 1, 2001, pp. 199–227.

Lather, Patti, and Chris Smithies. *Troubling the Angels: Women Living with HIV/AIDS*. Routledge, 1997.

Leonard, Rebecca Lorimer. "Traveling Literacies: Multilingual Writing on the Move." *Research in the Teaching of English*, vol. 48, no. 1, 2013, pp. 13–39.

———. *Writing on the Move: Migrant Women and the Value of Literacy.* U of Pittsburgh P, 2017.

Leonard, Rebecca Lorimer, et al. "Special Editors' Introduction to Issue 3.3." *Literacy in Composition Studies*, vol. 3, no. 3, 2015, pp. vi–xii.

Levitt, Peggy, and Nina Glick Schiller. "Conceptualizing Simultaneity: A Transnational Social Field Perspective on Society." *International Migration Review*, vol. 38, no. 3, 2004, pp. 1002–39.

Lu, Min-Zhan. "Afterword: Reading Literacy Research against the Grain of Fast Capitalism." *Women and Literacy: Local and Global Inquiries for a New Century*, edited by Beth Daniell and Peter Mortensen. Lawrence Erlbaum Associates/NCTE, 2007, pp. 297–318.

———. "Living-English Work." *College English*, vol. 68, no. 6, 2006, pp. 605–18.

Lu, Min-Zhan, and Bruce Horner. "The Problematic of Experience: Redefining Critical Work in Ethnography and Pedagogy." *College English*, vol. 60, no. 3, 1998, pp. 257–77.

Lugones, María. "Playfulness, 'World'-Travelling, and Loving Perception." *Hypatia*, vol. 2, no. 2, 1987, pp. 3–19.

Madison, D. Soyini. *Critical Ethnography: Methods, Ethics, and Performance.* 2nd ed., SAGE Publications, 2012.

March, Kathryn S. *"If Each Comes Halfway": Meeting Tamang Women in Nepal.* Cornell UP, 2002.

Meyers, Susan V. *Del Otro Lado: Literacy and Migration across the US-Mexico Border.* Southern Illinois UP, 2014.

Mohanty, Chandra Talpade. *Feminism without Borders: Decolonizing Theory, Practicing Solidarity.* Duke UP, 1992.

Moraga, Cherríe, and Gloria Anzaldúa. "Entering the Lives of Others: Theory in the Flesh." *This Bridge Called My Back: Writings by Radical Women of Color*, fortieth anniversary ed., edited by Moraga and Anzaldúa, SUNY P, 2021, pp. 17–19.

Morton, Stephen. *Gayatri Spivak: Ethics, Subalternity and the Critique of Postcolonial Reason.* Polity, 2007.

Narayan, Kirin. *Alive in the Writing: Crafting Ethnography in the Company of Chekhov.* U of Chicago P, 2012.

———. "Ethnography and Fiction: Where Is the Border?" *Anthropology and Humanism*, vol. 24, no. 2, 1999, pp. 134–47.

———. *Everyday Creativity: Singing Goddesses in the Himalayan Foothills.* U of Chicago P, 2016.

———. "Tools to Shape Texts: What Creative Nonfiction Can Offer Ethnography." *Anthropology and Humanism*, vol. 32, no. 2, 2007, pp. 130–44.

Nolin, Catherine. *Transnational Ruptures: Gender and Forced Migration*. Ashgate, 2006.

Pandey, Iswari P. *South Asian in the Mid-South: Migrations of Literacies*. U of Pittsburgh P, 2015.

Perry, Kristen H. "From Storytelling to Writing: Transforming Literacy Practices among Sudanese Refugees." *Journal of Literacy Research*, vol. 40, no. 3, 2008, pp. 317–58.

———. "Sharing Stories, Linking Lives: Literacy Practices among Sudanese Refugees." *Cultural Practices of Literacy: Case Studies of Language, Literacy, Social Practice, and Power*, edited by Victoria Purcell-Gates, Routledge, 2007, pp. 57–84.

Perry, Kristen H., and Annie Homan. "'What I Feel in My Heart': Literacy Practices of and for the Self among Adults with Limited or No Schooling." *Journal of Literacy Research*, vol. 46, no. 4, 2014, pp. 422–54.

Pollock, Della. "The Performative 'I'." *Cultural Studies—Critical Methodologies*, vol. 7, no. 3, 2007, pp. 239–55.

Rajouria, Aryaa. "She Married Young (The Lives Our Mothers Lived)." These Fine Lines: Poems of Restraint and Abandon, edited by Itsha Giri, Safu, Ekantakuna, 2016, p. 40.

Rana, Chandra. *Comprehensive Nepali: Speaking and Writing*. 2011.

Restaino, Jessica. *Surrender: Feminist Rhetoric and Ethics in Love and Illness*. Southern Illinois UP, 2019.

Robinson-Pant, Anna. *Why Eat Green Cucumbers at the Time of Dying? Women's Literacy and Development in Nepal*. UNESCO Institute for Education, 2000.

———. "Women and Literacy: A Nepal Perspective." *International Journal of Educational Development*, vol. 20, no. 4, 2000, pp. 349–64.

———, editor. *Women, Literacy, and Development: Alternative Perspectives*. Routledge, 2004.

Rosenberg, Lauren. *The Desire for Literacy: Writing in the Lives of Adult Learners*. CCCC/NCTE, 2015.

Royster, Jacqueline Jones. "When the First Voice You Hear Is Not Your Own." *College Composition and Communication*, vol. 47, no. 1, 1996, pp. 29–40.

Russo, Mary. *The Female Grotesque: Risk, Excess and Modernity*. Routledge, 1994.

Schiller, Nina Glick, et al. "From Immigrant to Transmigrant: Theorizing Transnational Migration." *Anthropological Quarterly*, vol. 68, no. 1, 1995, pp. 48–63.

Schrock, Richelle D. "The Methodological Imperatives of Feminist Ethnography." *Journal of Feminist Scholarship*, vol. 5, no. 5, 2013, pp. 54–60.

Seidman, Irving. *Interviewing as Qualitative Research: A Guide for Researchers in Education and the Social Sciences*. 5th edition, Teachers College P, 2019.

Shrestha, Tina. *Working the Paper: Nepali Suffering Narration, Compassion, and the US Asylum Process*. 2014. Cornell U, PhD dissertation.

Shuman, Amy. *Other People's Stories: Entitlement Claims and the Critique of Empathy*. U of Illinois P, 2005.

Silvester, Katie. "At the 'Ends of Kinship': Women Re(kin)figuring Literacy Practices in Protracted Displacement." *Literacy in Composition Studies*, vol. 10, no. 2, 2023, pp. 38–60.

Simon, Kaia. "Daughters Learning from Fathers: Migrant Family Literacies That Mediate Borders." *Literacy in Composition Studies*, vol. 5, no. 1, 2017, pp. 1–20.

Singh, Kamlesh, et al. "The Concept and Measure of *Sukha-Dukha*: An Indian Perspective on Well-Being." *Journal of Spirituality in Mental Health*, vol. 19, no. 2, 2017, pp. 116–32.

Sommer, Doris. "No Secrets: Rigoberta's Guarded Truth." *Women's Studies*, vol. 20, 1991, pp. 51–72.

Spivak, Gayatri Chakravorty. "Acting Bits/Identity Talk." *Critical Inquiry*, vol. 18, no. 4, 1992, pp. 770–803.

———. *A Critique of Postcolonial Reason: Toward a History of the Vanishing Present*. Harvard UP, 1999.

———. "Afterword." In *Imaginary Maps: Three Stories by Mahasweta Devi*, translated by Spivak, Routledge, 1995, pp. 197–205.

———. *In Other Worlds: Essays in Cultural Politics*. Methuen, 1987.

———. *The Postcolonial Critic: Interview, Strategies, Dialogues*. Edited by Sarah Harasym, Routledge, 1990.

———. "Responsibility." *boundary 2*, vol. 21, no. 3, 1994, pp. 19–64.

———. "Righting Wrongs." *Human Rights, Human Wrongs: The Oxford Amnesty Lectures 2001*, edited by Nicholas Owen. Oxford UP, 2003, pp. 164–227.

Spry, Tami. "A 'Performative-I' Copresence: Embodying the Ethnographic Turn in Performance and the Performative Turn in Ethnography," *Text and Performance Quarterly*, vol. 26, no. 4, 2006, 339–46.

Street, Brian V. "Futures of the Ethnography of Literacy?" *Language and Education*, vol. 18, no. 4, 2004, pp. 326–30.

———. *Literacy in Theory and Practice*. Cambridge UP, 1984.

———. "What's 'New' in New Literacy Studies? Critical Approaches to Literacy in Theory and Practice." *Current Issues in Comparative Education*, vol. 5, no. 2, 2003, pp. 77–91.

Stuckey, J. Elspeth. *The Violence of Literacy*. Boynton/Cook Publishers, 1991.

Trinh T. Minh-ha. *Elsewhere, within Here: Immigration, Refugeeism and the Boundary Event*. Routledge, 2011.

Tsing, Anna Lowenhaupt. *The Mushroom at the End of the World: On the Possibility of Life in Capitalist Ruins*. Princeton UP, 2021.

Turner, Ralph Lilley, and Dorothy Rivers Turner. *A Comparative and Etymological Dictionary of the Nepali Language*. Routledge and K. Paul, 1965.

United States. Dept. of Health and Human Services. Office of Refugee Resettlement. "Refugee Arrival Data." 24 Nov. 2015, hhs.gov, acf.hhs.gov/archive/orr/data/refugee-arrival-data.

———. *Report to the Congress FY 2012*. United States Office of Refugee Resettlement, 2013.

———. *Office of Refugee Resettlement Year in Review–FY 2013*. United States Office of Refugee Resettlement, 2013.

Vieira, Kate. *American by Paper: How Documents Matter in Immigrant Literacy*. U of Minnesota P, 2016.

———. "Writing about Others Writing: Some Fieldnotes." *Rhetorics Elsewhere and Otherwise: Contested Modernities, Decolonial Visions*, edited by Romeo García and Damián Baca. CCCC/NCTE, 2019, pp. 49–61.

———. *Writing for Love and Money: How Migration Drives Literacy Learning in Transnational Families*. Oxford UP, 2019.

Visweswaran, Kamala. *Fictions of Feminist Ethnography*. U of Minnesota P, 1994.

Warriner, Doris S. "Multiple Literacies and Identities: The Experiences of Two Women Refugees." *Women's Studies Quarterly*, vol. 32, nos. 1–2, 2004, pp. 179–95.

———. "Transnational Literacies: Immigration, Language Learning and Identity." *Linguistics and Education*, vol. 18, nos. 3–4, 2007, pp. 201–14.

INDEX

Abi Maya, 64, 65, 66, 67, 85, 86, 100, 109–110, 119
   background, 49–51
   "The Hungry Shepherd Died" (*Gothalā Bhōkalā Māralā*), 49
absence
   literacy stories as stories of, 74, 75–85, 85–91
   living-English stories as stories of, 66–67, 74, 113
absence, literacy. *See also* literacy, denial of
   and the experience of absence, 85–87
   history of, 82–85
   as a literacy act, 84–85
   women's stories of, purpose in, 91–92
accumulation economy, 9
accumulation theory of literacy, 6, 8, 25, 74, 91, 114
agency, literate, 8, 91–92
aging constraint on learning English, xvii, 16, 52, 54–55, 57, 62–63, 65, 87–88, 104–105
Alcoff, Linda, 21
Amashi, 96–98, 101
Ambika, 76–77
Anzaldúa, Gloria, 19, 67

Baca, Damián, xvii, 18
Behar, Ruth, xvii, 26
Beldangi II Spoken English Center, 96–99

Bhagat, 102
Bhutan
   the agitation, reflections on, 50–52
   census of 1988, 11–12, 46, 130n3
   Citizenship Act of 1977, 10–11
   conflict in, 35
   demonstrations of resistance in, 11–12
   education in, 13, 33–35, 40–42, 45, 52, 55–56, 66–67, 109
   integration of Nepali-speaking Bhutanese citizens, 10
   Nationality Law of 1958, 10, 11
   returning to, possibility of, 12, 35–36
   voluntary emigration program, 12
   work in, 41–42, 45, 49–52, 109
Bhutanese, ancestry, 10, 85
Bhutanese Mutual Assistance Association of Tucson (BMAAT), 4, 95
Bhutanese of Nepali origin in Bhutan, 10–12
Bhutanese Refugee Education Program, Caritas Nepal, 4–5
Bhutanese refugee resettlement program, US, 3
body language, 87
Brandt, Deborah, 6–7

Calafell, Bernadette, 18–19
capital accumulation theory, 6, 9
cardamom, 108–109

Caritas Nepal, Bhutanese Refugee Education Program, 4–5
Caritas Nepal Spoken English Centers, 13–14, 33
children as a constraint on learning, xv, 33, 36, 48, 63, 87, 105
citizenship, 76, 93–95
collaboration, contamination as, 26, 31
community, language classes for, 8, 102
community listening, 22–23
complicity, tracing, 110
connection. *See also* friendship
  language classes for, xv–xvi, 14, 16–17, 74–75, 109, 116–118
  in living-English stories, 107
  in singing and dancing together, 74, 93–100
contamination as collaboration, 26, 31
cultural attitudes constraining learning, 14, 57, 102, 131n3
Cushman, Eleanor, xvii, 18

date waiting, indefinite time of, 13, 25, 44, 80
"Decolonizing Community Writing with Community Listening: Story, Transrhetorical Resistance, and Indigenous Cultural Literacy Activism" (Jackson & DeLaune), 22
DeLaune, Dorothy Whitehorse, 22–23
Department of Economic Security, AZ, 4
The Desire for Literacy: Writing in the Lives of Adult Learners (Rosenberg), 17
"The Desire to Learn" (*Siknē Icch*ā) (Susmita), 32–33
Devika, 109
Durga, 94–96, 101–102, 107

education in Bhutan, denial of, 13, 33–35, 40–42, 45, 52, 55–56, 66–67
"Elephants Don't Get Big by Reading" (*Hāttī PaDhēra Thulo Hudaina*), 74, 75–85, 83–84
employment, learning English for, 76–77, 83–84
English language
  beliefs around the, 87
  hope and violence of, xix
ethics
  of listening and (re)telling, 21–26
  of nonmastery, 110
  setting to work as an engagement in, 75
  of speaking with/to, xix
  story, 16
ethnographic research, harm done by, 22
ethnography, a performance of possibilities, 19–20

family, as a reason to learn English, 40, 53, 59, 76
fear, learning English to overcome, 51, 52
freedom, as a reason to learn English, 54
friendship. *See also* connection, language classes for
  after resettlement, 95–96
  effects of caste and language differences on, 98–99
  language classes and, 48, 106
  learning as a performance of, 74
  "We Will Play (Sing and Dance) Sangīnī" ((*Hamī Sangīnī Khēlnēchaum*)), 74, 93–100

García, Romeo, xvii, 18
garden school, 96–98, 101, 107
Geeta, 80–83, 103

Globalizing Literacies and Identities: Translingual and Transcultural Literacy Practices of Bhutanese Refugees in the US (Lamsal), 17
Gopal, 93–95, 102
Gorkhali reign, 10

happiness
  collectively experienced, 106–107
  and grief, a life of, 104
  in language classes, 14
hope and violence of literacy, xix, 9, 15–16, 30, 106–107
hun, 67
"The Hungry Shepherd Died" (*Gothalā Bhōkalā Māralā*) (Abi Maya), 49
husbands, 45–46, 57, 102

identities-in-motion, 67–68
identity, nonliterate, 65, 67, 74, 91
"I Learn for Myself" (*Ma aphnai Lāgi Sikchu*) (Suk Maya), 39–40
Imaginary Maps: Three Stories by Mahasweta Devi (Spivak), 73
independence, learning English for, 45, 64
Indigenous Rai, appearance, xiv–xv
"It Happened with Love" (*Māyā Sanga Bhayō*), 116–118

Jackson, Rachel, 22–23
Januka, 76–78, 83–84, 86, 90
"Just a Little (English) Comes (To Me)" ((*Malaaī*) *Ali-ali (Angrējī) Āuchha*)) (Kali Maya), 44

Kali Maya, 64–65, 65, 66–68, 101, 103–107, 119
  background, 45–46
  date waiting, 44
  "Just a Little (English) Comes (To Me)" ((*Malaaī*) *Ali-ali (Angrējī) Āuchha*)), 44

resettlement process, 46
  self-described, 44–45
Kamal, 86
Kausila, 65, 66, 67, 101, 103–108, 117–118, 119
"(Learning English) is just like the Joys and Sorrows of Home" (*Gharkō Sukha-dukha Jastai Hō*), 54
  background, 55
  current life of, 62
  on desire to learn, 55–59, 62
  kinship found in literacy classes, 98–99, 102
Kiowa listening/storytelling practices, 22
Kirat, xiv
knowledge-making
  learning to learn vs., 21
  living-English stories effect on, 29
  personal experience in, 19
  sangīnī as a space of women's, 74, 93–100, 103
Kynard, Carmen, 18–19

Lamsal, Tika, 17–18
learning
  a negotiation of hope and violence, 106–107
  between novice and expert, 108–113
  occasions and motivations, proliferation of print and, 6
  tensions and contradictions in value of, 91
learning at the time to die, xiii, 14, 36, 111
learning English
  commitment to, 14, 39–41, 43–44, 48–49, 58, 65, 90, 111
  learning Nepali vs., 56–57
  a performance of possibilities, 103–107
  possibility of, 85

pride in, 34, 64
promises vs. constraints of, 16
struggle in, xiii, 84–85, 88–90, 105–106
learning English, constraints on
  aging, xvii, 16, 52, 54–55, 57, 62–63, 65, 87–88, 104–105
  children, 36
  cultural, 14
  employment, 94
  forgetting, xv, 39, 44, 52, 54–55, 105
  shyness, 81–82
learning English, reasons for
  citizenship, 76, 93–95
  collective, 106
  community, 8, 102
  connection, xv–xvi, 14, 16–17, 74–75, 109, 116–118
  a creative response to tensions shaping an uncertain future, 8–9
  desire, 8–9, 36, 55–59, 62–63
  employment, 76–77, 83–84
  family, 40, 53, 59, 76
  fear, 51, 52
  freedom, 54
  friendship, 48, 106
  friend's recommendation, 33
  happiness found, 14
  to imagine an-other world of learning, 30
  independence, 45, 64
  intrinsic, 106
  love shared, xv–xvi, 106, 117
  mobility, 14
  name writing, 33–34, 37, 64, 87, 88–89, 106
  oppression, resisting, 105–106
  resettlement, 8, 14, 32–34, 36–38, 40–41, 48–49, 53, 58, 62–63, 65, 87–89, 104
  solidarity, 8, 14, 102–103, 110
  speaking with/to a shared responsibility, 17
  survival, 14, 41, 64, 109–110
  understanding others, 76–77, 83–84
  "(Learning English) is just like the Joys and Sorrows of Home" (*Gharkō Sukha-dukha Jastai Hō*) (Kausila), 54
learning Nepali
  but forgetting, 44, 105
  language classes described, 102
  learning English vs., 56–57
  Silvester, 60
  struggle in, xiii–xiv, xv, 48
  usefulness of, 41, 62, 63, 87, 101
learning Nepali, constraints on
  children, xv, 33, 48, 63, 87, 105
  cultural attitudes, 57, 102, 131n3
  husbands, 102
  purposelessness, feeling of, 45, 105
  shame, 57
  time, xv
learning to learn
  from living-English stories, 69, 73–75
  meaning of, 21, 75
  by speaking with and to, 30
  toward and ethics of listening/(re)telling, 21–26
Leonard, Rebecca Lorimer, 7
listening
  community, 22–23
  effectively, possibility of, 110
  ethics-centered, noncoercive, 17
  loving perception practice in, 91
  rhetorical, 17
  shared responsibility, 22–23
listening and (re)telling
  a coperformance and performance of possibility, 15–21
  ethics of, 21–26
"Listening Back" (Silvester), 59–60, 66–68
literacy
  as accumulation, 6, 8, 25, 74, 91
  agency and, 8
  beliefs around, 65

desire for, 104
gendered and sexed practices of, 13, 35, 40–42, 45, 66–68
hope and violence of, xix, 9, 15–16, 30, 83, 106–107
investments in literacy-economies of literacy relationship, 9
mattering of, 68
meaning of, 15
parable about the limits and consequences of (il)literacy, 86
for survival, xiv, 14, 41, 89
tensions and contradictions in value of, 91
literacy, denial of. *See also* violence and hope of literacy
as an absent presence, 74
Bhutan, 13, 33–35, 40–42, 45, 52, 55–56, 66–67
gendered and sexed practices of, 13, 35, 40–42, 45
literacy classes. *See also* learning English
ambivalence and ambiguity toward, 64–65
encouraging attendance to, 80–81, 84
kinship found in, 98–99, 102
questioning the value of, 100
reasons for dwindling attendance, 81–83
target audience, age of, 102
us vs. them dynamic in attending, 84
literacy learning, transnational economy of literacy influencing, 6
meaning of, 75
promises vs. reality of, 15–16, 18, 112
purpose of, 8–9
reframing, 9, 15, 25, 73, 116
scholarship on, 8–9
as stories of absence, 90–91
literacy myth of the literate subject, 68
literacy sponsorship, 6–7

literacy success, 25
living-English stories
across languages sites of learning and time, 68–69, 73–75
ambivalence and ambiguity in, 64–65
belonging created with, 107
commonalities across, 65–68
"The Desire to Learn" (*Siknē Icch*ā) (Susmita), 32–33
an effect of knowledge production, 29
function of, 29–30
identities, narrating and reforming of multiple and shifting in migration, 83
identities-in-motion in, 67–68
"I Learn for Myself" (*Ma aphnaī Lāgi Sikchu*) (Suk Maya), 39–40
importance of, 16
kindred and community ties in, 107
a knowledge of moving literacies in, 29
learning to learn from, 69, 73–75
lessons in, 113–116
listening back, 59–60, 66–68
meaning of, xviii, 15
a performance of possibilities, 107
resiting through snapshots, time lapses, and analysis, 68–69
solidarity and connection in, 107
as stories of absence, 66–67, 113
tension in, 29, 68
truth of, 61–63
women's insistence on nonliteracy in, 67, 74
living stories, 16
love
learning English, reasons for, xv–xvi, 106, 117
learning with, xv–xvi, 106, 117
listening with, 91
singing and dancing, talking and laughing together with, 74, 93–100

stories of, 101
loving perception, 91, 117–118
Lu, Min-Zhan, xviii, 29
Lugones, María, 91

Madison, D. Soyini, 19–20
Manju, 80
migrant literacy, sociomaterial theory of, 7–8
Minh-ha, Trinh T., 60–61, 128n4
mobility
  inequalities in defined by choice, 7
  learning English, reasons for, 14
Mon Maya, 78–79, 84, 90
Moraga, Cherríe, 19, 67
motion, literacy in. *See also* literacy learning, transnational
  Amashi's adult education, 96–98, 101
  constraints on, 6
  Durga's garden, 96–98, 101
  learning to learn from, 116–118
  products and processes of, 7–8
  "We Will Play (Sing and Dance) Sangīnī" (*(Hamī Sangīnī Khēlnēchaum)*), 74, 93–100
  word work defining, 7
moving literacies
  learning to learn from, 116–118
  living-English stories indexing, xix
  meaning of, 116–117
  purpose of, 108

name writing, learning English for, 33–34, 37, 64, 87, 88–89, 106
Nepal, Gorkhali reign, 10
Nepali-speaking Bhutanese, emigration to and integration in Nepal, 12. *See also* refugees
Nepali Terai region, xv
Nepal refugee camps. *See* resettlement camps
Nima, 109
Nor Maya, 81

observer, the vulnerable, xvii
Office of Refugee Resettlement, US, 4
oppression, resisting through English learning, 105–106
Oxfam literacy program, 33, 44–45, 48, 52, 55–57, 63, 87, 101–102, 105

Pabi, 78–79
Pandey, Iswari P., 6–7, 15, 29
Parbati, xvii
performance of possibilities
  ethnography as a, 19–20
  learning English a, 103–107
  listening and (re)telling as, 15–21
  sangīnī as, 107
  storytelling as a, 15–21, 107
performance studies, 19
Pima County Community College Adult Education Refugee Education Project, 3
power dynamics, ethnographic harm in, 22
"The Problem of Speaking for Others" (Alcoff), 21
Puspa, 81–82

realities, re-thinking transnational, 61–66
refugees. *See also* resettlement camps
  adult education opportunities, 33
  integration in Nepal, 12
  language training, focus of, 5
  medical care, 46–47
  refusal to leave Nepal, 9–10
  repatriation possibilities, 12, 35–36
  resettlement questions, 9–10
  statistics, 10, 12
refugees, women. *See also* learning English
  described, xiv–xv
  husbands, 45–46, 57
  images of US, 38–39, 47
  on importance of education, 36–37

life of happiness and grief, 104
living conditions, 38
marriage, stories of, 51
persistence through adversity, 14, 39–41, 43–44, 48–49, 58, 65, 90, 111
reasons for not leaving, 43
self-described, 104–106
self-identified as illiterate, 65, 67, 74, 91
women's literacy learning through solidarity, 103
relationships
ethical, formation of, 20, 22
learning English, reasons for, xv–xvi, 14, 16–17, 48, 74–75, 106, 109, 116–118
sangīnī as a performance of knotting, 107
resettlement
date waiting, indefinite time of, 13, 25, 44, 80
imagining, 59
language of, 14
learning English for, 8, 14, 32–34, 36–38, 40–41, 48–49, 53, 58, 62–63, 65, 87–89, 104
life before and after, threads connecting, 108
medical evaluations, 46, 130n5
process, 12–13
US programs for, 3–4
resettlement, after
citizenship classes, 93–95
Durga's garden, 96–98, 101
goals for learning/goals for life, 77, 79
language and literacy training programs, 3–4, 76–78
learning English, 76–77, 84, 106
life, 95–96
refugee images of, 38–39, 47
work, worries about, 39, 47, 53, 76–77, 87

resettlement, conditions restricting
drug use, 46
incarceration, 44, 105
lying during interview, 47
marriage to a local, 62
special needs, 105
resettlement camps. *See also* refugees
adult education opportunities, 33
camp leaders, connecting with, 4–5
described, 9, 79–80
establishment of, 12
life in, 97–98
living conditions, 38
medical care, 46–47
returning to the, 119–120
statistics, 12
work for women in, 42, 82
(re)telling
a coperformance and performance of possibility, 15–21
ethics of, 21–26
rhetorical studies, 19
Rosenberg, Lauren, 17–18
Royster, Jacqueline Jones, 26

Sabitra, 76–77, 83, 90
sangīnī
performance of knotting of relationship, 107
performance of possibilities, 107
a space of women's knowledge production, 103
stories as a form of, 106, 113, 119–120
"We Will Play (Sing and Dance) Sangīnī" ((*Hamī Sangīnī Khēlnēchaum*)), 74, 93–100
Seti Maya, 109
shame as a constraint on learning, 57
shepherd, story of the (*go Thalā bhkalā*), 49–50, 85–86, 91, 109–110
sign language, 34, 37, 64, 87, 89

Silvester, Katie
  about, xv
  farewell ceremony for, 99–100
  interpreters, collaboration with, 18
  language skills, xiii–xiv, 60
  "Listening Back," 59–60, 66–68
  listening back, 113–116
  in Nepal, 60–61
  reflections, 110–113
  research methods, 121–126
  return to the camps, 119–120
  transnational realities, re-thinking, 61–66
  vulnerable observer, xv
  writing of narrative encounters, goal of, 31
singing and dancing, a space of women's knowledge production, 74, 93–100, 103
sociomaterial theory of migrant literacy, 7–8
solidarity
  in English learning, 8, 14, 102–103, 110
  in living-English stories, 107
  in singing and dancing together, 74, 93–100
speaking nearby, 128n4
speaking with/to, 15–21, 30
Spivak, Gayatri Chakravorty, 20, 73, 75, 110
stories, listening to and (re)telling
  a coperformance and performance of possibility, 15–21
  ethics of, 21–26
storytelling
  to imagine an-other world of learning, 30
  listener/teller dynamics, 23
  a performance of possibilities, 15–21, 107
  as remembering, reprocessing, and reinterpreting of literacy experience, 105
  as a response to the violence of literacy, 16, 30
  as *sangīnī*, *106, 113, 119–120*
subjects of the performance, researchers' responsibility to, 20
sukha-dukha, 106–107
Suk Maya, 64–65, 66–68, 89–90, 100, 119–120
  background, 40–42
  "I Learn for Myself" (*Ma aphnaī Lāgi Sikchu*), 39–40
  on learning English, 61–62
  resettlement process, 40
survival, learning English for, 14, 41, 64, 109–110
Susmita, xiii–xvi, 8–10, 13–14, 16, 63–65, 66–68, 67, 87–89, 100, 110–111, 119–120
  biography, 33–39
  "The Desire to Learn" (*Siknē Icch*ā), 32–33

teachers of English, 40, 90, 96–97
Thalu, 80
theory in the flesh, 19, 67, 106
Tibetan-Nepalese ethnic groups, xiv
Tij festivities, 107
translations and transcriptions, 17–18, 21
translators, 18
transnational literacies. *See also* literacy learning, transnational
  Amashi's adult education, 96–98, 101
  Durga's garden, 96–98, 101
  purpose of, 8–9
Trapped by Inequality: Bhutanese Refugee Women in Nepal, 12qr
Tsing, Anna, 26, 31
Tulasi, 108, 110

Vieira, Kate, 7, 22–23
violence and hope of literacy, xix, 9, 15–16, 30, 106–107

"We Will Play (Sing and Dance) Sangīnī" (*(Hamī Sangīnī Khēlnēchaum)*), 74, 93–100
wonder and loss, collectively experienced, 106–107
word work, 7, 16–17, 29
work
   after resettlement, 39, 47, 53, 87
   in Bhutan, 41–42, 45, 49–52, 109
   setting to, 75
   for women in resettlement camps, 42, 82
"Writing about Others Writing" (Vieira), 22
writing legacy of abuse, 22

AUTHOR

Katie Silvester is an associate professor of English and coordinator of multilingual writing at Indiana University Bloomington. Her work appears in *Literacy in Composition Studies* and in the edited collections *Critical Views on Teaching and Learning English around the Globe: Qualitative Research Approaches*, edited by José Aldemar Álvarez V. et al.; *Contested Spaces of Teaching and Learning: Practitioner Ethnographies of Adult Education in the United States*, edited by Janise Hurtig and Carolyn Chernoff; and *Plurilingual Pedagogies for Multilingual Classrooms: Engaging the Rich Communicative Repertoires of U.S. Students*, edited by Kay M. Losey and Gail Shuck.

BOOKS IN THE CCCC STUDIES IN WRITING & RHETORIC SERIES

Living English, Moving Literacies: Women's Stories of Learning between the US and Nepal
Katie Silvester

Recollections from an Uncommon Time: 4C20 Documentarian Tales
Edited by Julie Lindquist, Bree Straayer, and Bump Halbritter

Transfer in an Urban Writing Ecology: Reimagining Community College–University Relations in Composition Studies
Christie Toth with Joanne Castillo, Nic Contreras, Kelly Corbray, Nathan Lacy, Westin Porter, Sandra Salazar-Hernandez, and Colleagues

Teachers Talking Writing: Perspectives on Places, Pedagogies, and Programs
Shane A. Wood

Materiality and Writing Studies: Aligning Labor, Scholarship, and Teaching
Holly Hassel and Cassandra Phillips

Salt of the Earth: Rhetoric, Preservation, and White Supremacy
James Chase Sanchez

Rhetorics of Overcoming: Rewriting Narratives of Disability and Accessibility in Writing Studies
Allison Harper Hitt

Writing Accomplices with Student Immigrant Rights Organizers
Glenn Hutchinson

Counterstory: The Rhetoric and Writing of Critical Race Theory
Aja Y. Martinez

Writing Programs, Veterans Studies, and the Post-9/11 University: A Field Guide
Alexis Hart and Roger Thompson

Beyond Progress in the Prison Classroom: Options and Opportunities
Anna Plemons

Rhetorics Elsewhere and Otherwise: Contested Modernities, Decolonial Visions
Edited by Romeo García and Damián Baca

Black Perspectives in Writing Program Administration: From the Margins to the Center
Edited by Staci M. Perryman-Clark and Collin Lamont Craig

Translanguaging outside the Academy: Negotiating Rhetoric and Healthcare in the Spanish Caribbean
Rachel Bloom-Pojar

Collaborative Learning as Democratic Practice: A History
Mara Holt

Reframing the Relational: A Pedagogical Ethic for Cross-Curricular Literacy Work
Sandra L. Tarabochia

Inside the Subject: A Theory of Identity for the Study of Writing
Raúl Sánchez

Genre of Power: Police Report Writers and Readers in the Justice System
Leslie Seawright

Assembling Composition
Edited by Kathleen Blake Yancey and Stephen J. McElroy

Public Pedagogy in Composition Studies
Ashley J. Holmes

From Boys to Men: Rhetorics of Emergent American Masculinity
Leigh Ann Jones

Freedom Writing: African American Civil Rights Literacy Activism, 1955–1967
Rhea Estelle Lathan

The Desire for Literacy: Writing in the Lives of Adult Learners
Lauren Rosenberg

On Multimodality: New Media in Composition Studies
Jonathan Alexander and Jacqueline Rhodes

Toward a New Rhetoric of Difference
Stephanie L. Kerschbaum

Rhetoric of Respect: Recognizing Change at a Community Writing Center
Tiffany Rousculp

After Pedagogy: The Experience of Teaching
Paul Lynch

Redesigning Composition for Multilingual Realities
Jay Jordan

Agency in the Age of Peer Production
Quentin D. Vieregge, Kyle D. Stedman, Taylor Joy Mitchell, and Joseph M. Moxley

Remixing Composition: A History of Multimodal Writing Pedagogy
Jason Palmeri

First Semester: Graduate Students, Teaching Writing, and the Challenge of Middle Ground
Jessica Restaino

Agents of Integration: Understanding Transfer as a Rhetorical Act
Rebecca S. Nowacek

Digital Griots: African American Rhetoric in a Multimedia Age
Adam J. Banks

The Managerial Unconscious in the History of Composition Studies
Donna Strickland

Everyday Genres: Writing Assignments across the Disciplines
Mary Soliday

The Community College Writer: Exceeding Expectations
Howard Tinberg and Jean-Paul Nadeau

A Taste for Language: Literacy, Class, and English Studies
James Ray Watkins

Before Shaughnessy: Basic Writing at Yale and Harvard, 1920–1960
Kelly Ritter

Writer's Block: The Cognitive Dimension
Mike Rose

Teaching/Writing in Thirdspaces: The Studio Approach
Rhonda C. Grego and Nancy S. Thompson

Rural Literacies
Kim Donehower, Charlotte Hogg, and Eileen E. Schell

Writing with Authority: Students' Roles as Writers in Cross-National Perspective
David Foster

Whistlin' and Crowin' Women of Appalachia: Literacy Practices since College
Katherine Kelleher Sohn

Sexuality and the Politics of Ethos in the Writing Classroom
Zan Meyer Gonçalves

African American Literacies Unleashed: Vernacular English and the Composition Classroom
Arnetha F. Ball and Ted Lardner

Revisionary Rhetoric, Feminist Pedagogy, and Multigenre Texts
Julie Jung

Archives of Instruction: Nineteenth-Century Rhetorics, Readers, and Composition Books in the United States
Jean Ferguson Carr, Stephen L. Carr, and Lucille M. Schultz

Response to Reform: Composition and the Professionalization of Teaching
Margaret J. Marshall

Multiliteracies for a Digital Age
Stuart A. Selber

Personally Speaking: Experience as Evidence in Academic Discourse
Candace Spigelman

Self-Development and College Writing
Nick Tingle

Minor Re/Visions: Asian American Literacy Narratives as a Rhetoric of Citizenship
Morris Young

A Communion of Friendship: Literacy, Spiritual Practice, and Women in Recovery
Beth Daniell

Embodied Literacies: Imageword and a Poetics of Teaching
Kristie S. Fleckenstein

Language Diversity in the Classroom: From Intention to Practice
Edited by Geneva Smitherman and Victor Villanueva

Rehearsing New Roles: How College Students Develop as Writers
Lee Ann Carroll

Across Property Lines: Textual Ownership in Writing Groups
Candace Spigelman

Mutuality in the Rhetoric and Composition Classroom
David L. Wallace and Helen Rothschild Ewald

The Young Composers: Composition's Beginnings in Nineteenth-Century Schools
Lucille M. Schultz

Technology and Literacy in the Twenty-First Century: The Importance of Paying Attention
Cynthia L. Selfe

Women Writing the Academy: Audience, Authority, and Transformation
Gesa E. Kirsch

Gender Influences: Reading Student Texts
Donnalee Rubin

Something Old, Something New: College Writing Teachers and Classroom Change
Wendy Bishop

Dialogue, Dialectic, and Conversation: A Social Perspective on the Function of Writing
Gregory Clark

Audience Expectations and Teacher Demands
Robert Brooke and John Hendricks

Toward a Grammar of Passages
Richard M. Coe

Rhetoric and Reality: Writing Instruction in American Colleges, 1900–1985
James A. Berlin

Writing Groups: History, Theory, and Implications
Anne Ruggles Gere

Teaching Writing as a Second Language
Alice S. Horning

Invention as a Social Act
Karen Burke LeFevre

The Variables of Composition: Process and Product in a Business Setting
Glenn J. Broadhead and Richard C. Freed

Writing Instruction in Nineteenth-Century American Colleges
James A. Berlin

Computers & Composing: How the New Technologies Are Changing Writing
Jeanne W. Halpern and Sarah Liggett

A New Perspective on Cohesion in Expository Paragraphs
Robin Bell Markels

Evaluating College Writing Programs
Stephen P. Witte and Lester Faigley

This book was typeset in Adobe Garamond Pro and
Myriad Pro by Barbara Frazier.
Typefaces used on the cover include Garamond
and News Gothic Standard.
The book was printed on 50-lb., white offset paper.